Python for Data Analysis

This book will introduce the learner to the basics of the python programming environment, including fundamental python programming techniques such as lambdas, reading and manipulating csv files, and the numpy library. The book will introduce data manipulation and cleaning techniques using the popular python pandas data science library and introduce the abstraction of the Series and DataFrame as the central data structures for data analysis, use functions such as groupby, matplotlib effectively. Different data visualisation tools like histograms, matplotlib are lucidly explained on real world data. It is a quick guide to learn Basic Python and Python for data analysis.

This book also aims to guide students of B.E. (Computer Science & Engineering) in performing practical and project work in python. It consist of chapter 1: Python Basic, Chapter 2: Functions, Packages and Classes, Chapter 3: Numpy & Matplotlib, Chapter 4: Pandas, Chapter 5: Solutions to Suggested programs, Mini Projects, Viva Question. Suggested Programs like Count Frequency of Words, Build Hungman Game, Plot a Graph, Data Cleaning & Operations and Mini Project like Recommender System, Twitter Sentimental Analysis, Linear Regression.

Dr. Latesh Malik,
Associate Professor,
Government College of Engineering, Nagpur

Dr. Sandhya Arora.
Professor,
Cummins College of Engineering for Women, Pune

Contents

Chapter 1: Python Basics

1.1	Python Features	1
1.2	Installation	2
1.3	Variable, statement and expression	3

    1.3.1 Comments
    1.3.2 Variables
        1.3.2.1 Identifier naming
        1.3.2.2 Data Types
    1.3.3 Statements
    1.3.4 Expressions
    1.3.5 Name spaces and scoping

1.4	Constants	9
1.5	Mathematical operators	9
1.6	Conditional and loop Statements	9

    1.6.1 If statement
    1.6.2 For statement
    1.6.3 Range() function
    1.6.4 Break & continue statement

1.7	Lists	12
1.8	Tuples	13
1.9	Sets	15
1.10	Dictionaries	16
1.11	Date & time	17

    1.11.1 Time tuple
    1.11.2 Getting current time
    1.11.3 Getting formatted time
    1.11.4 Getting calendar of a month

1.12	How to write python programs	19

    1.12.1 Logical & physical line
    1.12.2 Indentation

Chapter 2: Functions, Packages and Classes   22

2.1	Functions	22
2.2	Built-in Functions	22

[Python for Data Analysis]

2.3 Function Arguments 24
    2.3.1 Default Argument Values
    2.3.2 Keyword Arguments
    2.3.3 Arbitrary Argument Lists
    2.3.4 Unpacking Argument Lists
2.4 Lambda Expressions 27
2.5 Regular Expressions 28
    2.5.1 Raw Python Strings
    2.5.2 Matching a String
    2.5.3 Capturing Groups
    2.5.4 Finding & Replacing String
2.6 Compiling a Pattern 31
2.7 Classes & Objects 31
    2.7.1 Creating Classes
    2.7.2 Objects & Instance Variable
    2.7.3 Accessing Attributes
    2.7.4 Built-in Class Attributes
    2.7.5 Creating Constructors
2.8 Destroying Objects 35
2.9 Class Inheritance 36
2.10 Overloading Methods 38
    2.10.1 Base Overloading Methods
    2.10.2 Data Hiding
2.11 Exception Handling 40
    2.11.1 Handling Exception
    2.11.2 Raising Exception
2.12 Modules 42
    2.12.1 The import Statement
    2.12.2 Locating Modules
2.13 Packages in Python 44

Chapter 3: Numpy and Matplotlib 46

    3.1 Arrays 46
    3.2 Numpy 47
        3.2.1 Getting Numpy
        3.2.2 2D Numpy
        3.2.3 Array Creation
        3.2.4 Printing Arrays
        3.2.5 Numpy Basic Array Operations
        3.2.6 Universal Functions
        3.2.7 Indexing, Slicing and Iterating

      3.2.8   Splitting as Array
      3.2.9   Statistical Functions
3.3 Matplotlib   57
      3.3.1   Getting Matplotlib
      3.3.2   Introduction to Matplotlib
      3.3.3   Simple Plot
      3.3.4   Figures, Subplots, Axes and Ticks

Chapter 4: Pandas   67

4.1 Installing Pandas   67
4.2 Object Creation, Selection & Indexing   67
      4.2.1   Object Creation Series & Data Frame
      4.2.2   Viewing Data/ Lookups Data Frames
      4.2.3   Sorting by an Axis
      4.2.4   Selection by Label
      4.2.5   Selecting on a Multi-axis by Label
      4.2.6   Selection by Position
4.3 Handling NaN Values   71
4.4 Mapping   72
4.5 Reading Files   74
4.6 Plot   75
4.7 JOINS   77
4.8 Histograms   78
4.9 Data Time Index   79
4.10 Group By   81
4.11 Aggregation   83

Chapter 5 Suggested Practices   86

5.1 Suggested Programs   86
      1. Count Frequency of Words
      2. Build Hungman Game
      3. Plot a Graph
      4. Data Cleaning & Operations
5.2 Mini Project   92
      1. Recommender System
      2. Twitter Sentimental Analysis
      3. Linear Regression
      4. Natural Language Tool Kit
5.3 Viva Questions   114

Chapter 1: Python Basics

1.1 Python Features

Python is a interpreted, interactive, object-oriented, and high-level programming language. It was created by Guido van Rossum during 1985- 1990. Python interpreter source code is available under the GNU General Public License (GPL).

Features of Python Programming

1. **A simple language which is easier to learn**
   Python has a very simple and elegant syntax. It's easier to read and write Python programs compared to other languages like: C++, .NET, C#. Python allows us to focus on the solution rather than syntax.
2. **Free and open-source**
   It can be used freely and distributed, even for commercial use. Python's source code is open source. Python has a large community improving it in each iteration.
3. **Portability**
   Python programs can be portable from one platform to another, and run it without any changes. It runs on almost all platforms including Windows, Mac OS X and Linux.
4. **Extensible and Embeddable**
   Python code is embeddable in other code in C/C++/Java. It is possible to combine pieces of C/C++ or other languages with Python code. This will give application high performance as well as scripting capabilities.
5. **A high-level, interpreted language**
   Unlike C/C++, programmer need not to worry about memory management, garbage collection in Python. At run time, it automatically converts source code to the language of computer on which it is running.
6. **Large standard libraries**
   Python has a number of standard libraries which makes easy to program since programmer need not to write all the code. For example: You can use MySQLdb library using import MySQLdb to connect MySQL database on a Web server.
7. **Object-oriented**
   Everything in Python is an object. Object oriented programming (OOP) concepts are applicable to Python too.

1.2 Installation

1.1.1 Installation on Windows

- Visit https://www.python.org/downloads/ and download the latest version.
- Make sure you check option Add Python 3.6 to PATH.
- To change install location, click on Customize installation
- If not checked, check Add Python to environment variables. This does the same thing as Add Python 3.6 to PATH on the first install screen.

1.1.2 Installation on GNU/Linux

- For GNU/Linux users, use your distribution's package manager to install Python 3, e.g. on Debian & Ubuntu: sudo apt-get update && sudo apt-get install python3.
- To verify, open the terminal by opening the Terminal application or by pressing Alt + F2 and entering gnome-terminal. If that doesn't work, please refer the documentation of your particular GNU/Linux distribution. Now, run python3 and ensure there are no errors.
- You can see the version of Python on the screen by running:
  $ python3 -V
  Python 3.6.0

Python shell script will be like:

You can directly execute commands on shell or use file menu to use an editor to create Python Programs and run by embedded menu.

1.3 Python Variables, Statement & Expressions

1.3.1 Comments

 # symbol is used to write comments and is mainly useful as notes for the reader of the program.
For example:
print('hello world') # Note that print is a function

1.3.2 Variable

Variables - their value can vary, i.e., you can store anything using a variable. Variables are parts of your computer's memory where you store some information. Unlike literal constants, you need some method of accessing these variables and hence names are given to them.

1.3.2.1 Identifier Naming

Variables are examples of identifiers. *Identifiers* are names given to identify *something*. Rules for naming identifiers are:
- The first character of the identifier must be a letter of the alphabet or an underscore (_).
- The rest of the identifier name can consist of letters, underscores (_) or digits (0-9).
- Identifier names are case-sensitive. For example, and mychar are *not* the same as myChar

- Examples of *valid* identifier names are i, name_2. Examples of *invalid* identifier names are 2name, my-name and >a1b2_c.

1.3.2.2 Data Types

Python does not requires type to be declared before use but variables can hold values of different types called *data types*. Commonly used data types are *int, float, str* and *bool*.

Numbers

Numbers are mainly of two types : integers and floats. An example of an integer is 3 which is just a whole number. Examples of floating point numbers are 3.23 and 52.3E-6. The E notation indicates powers of 10. To declare variables in Python:

```
>>> a = 2       # assign the integer value 2 to the variable a
>>> b = 3.0     # assign the decimal value 3.0 to the variable b
>>> c = '5'     # assign the string '5' to the variable c
>>> a + b       # adding two numbers
7.0
```

To determine the datatype of a variable:

```
>>> a = 2
>>> type(a)
<type 'int'>
>>> b = 3.0
<type 'float'>
>>> c = 'hello'
>>> type(c)
<type 'str'>
>>> d = False
>>> type(d)
<type 'bool'>
```

Conversion between Data Types

Use the following functions for conversion between data types: float(x), int(x), str(x) etc.

```
>>> a = 5           # int
>>> b = float(a)    # convert to float
>>> b
```

```
5.0
>>> c = str(a)      # convert to string
>>> c
'5'
>>> d = int(4.6)    # convert to int, take note of the round down
>>> d
4
```

Strings

A string is a *sequence* of *characters*. Strings are collection of words. A String in Python can be represented using single, Double, triple quote.

Single Quote

You can specify strings using single quotes such as 'my string'. All white space i.e. spaces and tabs, within the quotes, are preserved as it is.

Double Quotes

Strings in double quotes work exactly in the same way as strings in single quotes. An example is "What is your name?".

Triple Quotes

You can specify multi line strings using triple quotes   (""" or '''). You can use single quotes and double quotes within the triple quotes. An example is:

'''This is a multi line string. This is the first line.
This is the second line.
"What's your name?" I asked.
He said "Bond , James Bond."
'''

The format method

Format method is used to convert values to string and pass them as parameters to prepare dynamic strings. Save the following lines as a file str_format.py:

#assign values
age = 22
name = 'Swaroop'

#
print('{0} was {1} years old when he wrote this book'.format (name, age))
print('Why is {0} playing with python?'.format(name))

Output:
$ python str_format.py
Swaroop was 22 years old when he wrote this book
Why is Swaroop playing with python?

0,1 are index position for parameters in format.

Notice that we could have achieved the same using string concatenation:
name + ' is ' + str(age) + ' years old'

To prevent newline character from being printed, you can specify that it should end with no space:
    print('a', end='')
    print('b', end='')
    Output is:
    ab
Or you can end with a space:

    print('x', end=' ')
    print('y', end=' ')
    print('z')
    Output is:
    x y z

Escape Sequences

To include single quote (') in a string display you cannot specify 'What's your name?'
 You can specify the string as 'What\'s your name?'.
Another way of specifying this specific string would be "What's your name?" i.e. using double quotes.
If you want to write two line string One way is to use a triple-quoted string or you can use an escape sequence for the newline character - \n to indicate the start of a new line.
An example is:

'This is the first line \n This is the second line'

1.3.3 Statements

A statement is an instruction that the Python interpreter can execute. When you type a statement on the command line, Python executes it and displays the result, if there is one. The result of a print statement is a value. Assignment statements don't produce a result.

A script usually contains a sequence of statements. If there is more than one statement, the results appear one at a time as the statements execute.

For example, the script

>   print 1
>   x = 2
>   print x

produces the output

> 1
> 2

Again, the assignment statement produces no output.

1.3.4 Expressions

An expression is a combination of values, variables, and operators. If you type an expression on the command line, the interpreter evaluates it and displays the result:

>   >>> 1 + 1
>   2

Although expressions contain values, variables, and operators, not every expression contains all of these elements. A value all by itself is considered an expression, and so is a variable.

>   >>> 17
>   17
>   >>> x
>   2

Confusingly, evaluating an expression is not quite the same thing as printing a value.

>   >>> message = 'Hello, World!'
>   >>> message
>   'Hello, World!'
>   >>> print message

Hello, World!

When the Python interpreter displays the value of an expression, it uses the same format you would use to enter a value. In the case of strings, that means that it includes the quotation marks. But if you use a print statement, Python displays the contents of the string without the quotation marks.

In a script, an expression all by itself is a legal statement, but it doesn't do anything. The script

```
17
3.2
'Hello, World!'
1 + 1
```
produces no output at all.

1.3.5 Namespaces and Scoping

A namespace is a dictionary of variable names and their corresponding objects. There are two types of name spaces :local namespace and global namespace. If a local and a global variable have the same name, the local variable precedes the global variable.

Each function has its own local namespace. Class methods follow the same scoping rule as ordinary functions as in C++/Java. Python assumes that any variable assigned a value in a function is local.

In order to assign a value to a global variable in a function, use the global statement is required. The statement global x tells Python that x is a global variable. Python start searching the global namespace for the variable.

For example ,if we define a variable x in the global namespace. Within the function x, we assign x a value, therefore Python assumes x as a local variable. However, we accessed the value of the local variable x before setting it, so an UnboundLocalError is the result. Uncommenting the global statement fixes the problem.

```
#!/usr/bin/python
x = 2000
def Addx():
   # Uncomment the following line to fix the code:
   # global x
   x = x + 1
print x
Addx()
print x
```

1.4 Literal Constants

It is a *constant* because its value cannot be changed. An example of a literal constant is a number like 5, 1.23. String constant like 'This is a string' or "It's a string!".

1.5 Mathematical Operations

For numbers, the usual mathematical rules are applicable. Like : *, /, +, - on numbers.

```
>>> 1/2     # returns integer value
0
>>> 1/2.0   # returns decimal value
0.5
```
Take note of the following operations on string
```
>>> '1' + '2'   # concatenation instead of addition
'12'
>>> '1' * 5     # This is valid in Python
'11111'
```
Summary of Mathematical Operators

Symbols	Operations	Examples	Outputs
+	Addition	a = 1+2	3
-	Subtraction	a = 2-1	1
*	Multiplication	a = 2*2	4
/	Division	a = 5.0/2	2.5
//	Truncating Division	a = 5.0//2	2.0
%	Modulo	a = 5%2	1
**	Power	a = 5**2	25

1.6 Conditional & Loop Statement

1.6.1 *if* Statement

If statement is used for conditional and selected instructions execution. For example:

```
>>> x = int(input("Please enter an integer: "))
Please enter an integer: 43
```

```
>>> if x < 0:
...     x = 0
...     print('Negative changed to zero')
... elif x == 0:
...     print('Zero')
... elif x == 1:
...     print('Single')
... else:
...     print('More')
Output: More
```

There can be 0 or more elif parts, and the else part is optional. The keyword 'elif' is short form for 'else if', and is useful to avoid excessive indentation. An if ,elif , elif sequence is a substitute for the switch or case statements is found in other languages.

1.6.2 for Statement

The for statement in Python is giving the user the ability to define both the iteration step and halting condition , for statement iterates over the items of any sequence in the order in which they appear. For example :

```
>>> # Measure some strings:
... words = ['cat', 'window', 'defense']
>>> for w in words:
    print(w, len(w))
cat 3
window 6
defense 7
```

1.6.3 The range() Function

If you need to iterate over a sequence of numbers in list or range, the built-in function range() generates arithmetic progressions:

```
>>> for i in range(3):
...     print(i)
...
0
1
2
```

The given end point in range() is never part of the generated sequence; range(5) generates 5 values, the legal indices for items of a sequence of length 5. It is possible to let the range start at number other than 0, or to specify a different increment:

```
range(5, 10)
   5 through 9

range(-10, -100, -30)
   -10, -40, -70
```
To iterate over the indices of a sequence for loop can be used like:
```
>>> a = ['I', 'love', 'my', 'mom']
>>> for i in range(len(a)):
...     print(i, a[i])
```

Output:
0 I
1 love
2 my
3 mom

1.6.4 break and continue Statements

The break statement is used to exit from inner most loop and control goes to next instruction immediately after loop. Given below for/while loop searches for prime numbers. Loop in exited when number is divisible by any other number.

```
>>> for n in range(2, 10):
      for x in range(2, n):
        if n % x == 0:
          print(n, 'equals', x, '*', n//x)
          break
      else:
        print(n, 'is a prime number')
2 is a prime number
3 is a prime number
4 equals 2 * 2
```

The continue statement continues with the next iteration of the loop after skipping instructions after continue statement in a loop:

```
>>> for num in range(2, 5):
      if num % 2 == 0:
        print("Even number found", num)
        continue
      print("Number Found", num)
Even number found 2
```

[Python for Data Analysis]

Number Found 3
Even number found 4

1.7 Lists

List is *compound* data type which is used to group together other values. It can be written as a list of comma-separated values between square brackets. Lists may contain items of different type or same type.

```
>>> squares = [1, 4, 9, 16, 25]
>>> squares
[1, 4, 9, 16, 25]
```
Like strings sequence, lists can be indexed and sliced:
```
>>> squares[0]  # indexing returns the item at location zero
1
>>> squares[-1]
25
>>> squares[-3:]  # slicing returns a new list from -3 to -1
[9, 16, 25]
```

Indexing in list is circular and starting index is zero .Last item in list has index n-1 and -1, second last item has index n-2 and -2 and so on.
Slice operations return a new list consisting of requested elements. This means that the following slice returns a new copy(sub list) of the list.
```
>>> squares[:]
[1, 4, 9, 16, 25 ]
```
Lists also support operations like concatenation:
```
>>> squares + [36, 49, 64, 81, 100 ]
[1, 4, 9, 16, 25, 36, 49, 64, 81, 100 ]
```
Unlike strings, it is possible to change content of list:
```
>>> squares = [1, 4,9,15,25]]  # 15 is not square
>>> squares[3] = 16  # replace the 4**3
>>> squares
[1,4,9,16,25]
```
We can also add new items at the end of the list, by using the append() *method* .
```
>>> squares.append(36)  # add the square of 6
>>> squares
[1,4,9,16,25,36]
```
Assignment to slices is also possible, and this can even change the size of the list also.
```
>>> letters = ['a', 'b', 'c', 'd', 'e', 'f']
```

```
>>> letters
['a', 'b', 'c', 'd', 'e', 'f']
>>> # replace some values with new
>>> letters[2:4] = ['C', 'D']
>>> letters
['a', 'b', 'C', 'D', 'e', 'f']
>>> # now remove slice of items
>>> letters[2:5] = []
```

The built-in function len () also applies to lists:
```
>>> letters = ['a', 'b', 'c', 'd']
>>> len(letters)
4
```
It is possible to nest lists (list within list), for example:
```
>>> a = ['a', 'b']
>>> n = [1, 2]
>>> x = [a, n]
>>> x
[['a', 'b'], [1, 2]]
>>> x[0]
['a', 'b']
>>> x[0][1]
'b'
```

1.8 Tuples

A tuple is a sequence of immutable Python objects which cannot be changed unlike lists. Tuples are sequences, like lists. The differences between tuples and lists are, the tuples use parentheses, whereas lists use square brackets.

Creating a tuple is putting different comma-separated values. Optionally that can be put these comma-separated values between parentheses also. For example –

tup1 = ('physics', 'chemistry', 1997, 2000,2016);
tup2 = (1, 2, 3, 4, 5,6);
tup3 = "a", "b", "c", "d","e";

The empty tuple is written as two parentheses without any element –
tup1 = ();

To write a tuple consisting of a single value you have to include a comma
tup1 = (50,);

Tuple indices start at 0, and they can be sliced, concatenated, and so on like string indices.

1.8.1 Accessing Values in Tuples

To access values in tuple, use the square brackets for slicing along with the index to obtain value available at that index. For example –

```
#!/usr/bin/python
tup1 = ('physics', 'chemistry', 1997, 2000,2016);
tup2 = (1, 2, 3, 4, 5, 6, 7 ,8);

print "tup1[0]: ", tup1[0]
print "tup2[1:5]: ", tup2[1:5]
it produces the following result –
tup1[0]:  physics
tup2[1:5]:  [2, 3, 4, 5]
```

1.8.2 Updating Tuples

Tuples are immutable which means the values of tuple elements can't be changed. You are able to extract portions of existing tuples to create new tuples as the following example –

```
#!/usr/bin/python
tup1 = (12, 34.57);
tup2 = ('abc', 'xyzw');
# Following action is not valid
# tup1[0] = 100;
# Create a new tuple as follows
tup3 = tup1 + tup2;
print tup3
When the above code is executed, it produces the  result –
(12, 34.56, 'abc', 'xyzw')
```

1.8.3 Delete Tuple Elements

Removing individual tuple elements from collection is not possible. To explicitly remove an entire tuple, use the **del** statement. For example:

```
#!/usr/bin/python
tup = ('physics', 'chemistry', 1997, 2000,2016);
print tup
del tup;
print "After deleting tup : "
```

[Python for Data Analysis]

print tup

If above code is executed ,an exception raised, because after **del tup** tuple does not exist any more –

('physics', 'chemistry', 1997, 2000)
After deleting tup :
Traceback (most recent call last):
 File "test.py", line 9, in <module>
    print tup;
NameError: name 'tup' is not defined

1.9 Sets

A set is an unordered collection of elements with no duplicate. Basic operations on set are membership testing and eliminating duplicate entries. Other mathematical operations like union, intersection, difference, and symmetric difference can also be performed on set.
To create new set Curly braces or the set() function can be used. To create an empty set , use set(), not {} because the latter creates an empty dictionary.
Here is a brief demonstration:

```
>>> basket = {'apple', 'orange', 'apple', 'pear', 'orange', 'banana'}
>>> print(basket)       # duplicates have been removed
{'orange', 'banana', 'pear', 'apple'}
>>> 'orange' in basket    # membership testing True
>>> 'crabgrass' in basket   #Not member False
>>> # Set operations on two sets
>>> a = set('abracadabraabra')
>>> b = set('alacazamala')
>>> a                # print unique letters in a
{'a', 'r', 'b', 'c', 'd'}
>>> a - b              #print letters in a but not in b
{'r', 'd', 'b'}
>>> a | b              # print letters in either a or b
{'a', 'c', 'r', 'd', 'b', 'm', 'z', 'l'}
>>> a & b              # print letters in both a and b
{'a', 'c'}
>>> a ^ b            # print letters in a or b but not both
{'r', 'd', 'b', 'm', 'z', 'l'}
```

[Python for Data Analysis]

1.10 Dictionaries

A useful data type built into Python is the *dictionary*. Dictionaries are found in other languages as "associative memories" or "associative arrays". Unlike sequences, which are indexed by a range of numbers, dictionaries are indexed by *keys*. Dictionaries can be any immutable type.
 Tuples can be used as keys if they consist of only strings, numbers, or tuples(immutable objects). If a tuple consist of any mutable object either directly or indirectly, it cannot be used as a key. Lists can't be used as keys, since lists can be modified in place using index assignments, slice assignments, or methods like append() and extend().
Dictionary is an unordered set of *key: value* pairs. Keys are unique within a dictionary. A pair of braces {} creates an empty dictionary . Placing a comma-separated list of key:value pairs within the braces adds key:value pairs to the dictionary.
The main operations on a dictionary are storing a value with some key and extracting the value of the key. To delete a key:value pair with **del** command. If you store value of a key that is already in use, the old value associated with that key is forgotten. To extract a value using a non-existent key is an error.
 list(d.keys()) function on a dictionary returns a list of all the keys in an arbitrary order. To check whether a single key is in the dictionary or not, use the in keyword. Here is a small example using a dictionary:

```
>>> tel = {'jack': 4098, 'hena':4087, 'sape': 4139 }
>>> tel['guido'] =  4127
>>> tel
{'sape': 4139, 'guido': 4127, 'hena':4087, 'jack': 4098}
>>> tel['jack']
4098
>>> del tel['sape']
>>> tel['irv'] = 4127
>>> tel
{'guido': 4127, 'irv': 4127, 'hena':4087, 'jack': 4098}
>>> list(tel.keys())
['irv', 'guido', 'hena','jack']
>>> sorted(tel.keys())
['guido','hena', 'irv', 'jack']
>>> 'guido' in tel
True
>>> 'jack' not in tel
False
```

The constructor dict() builds dictionaries directly from sequences of key-value pairs:
>>> dict([('sape', 4139), ('guido', 4127), ('hena',4087)('jack', 4098)])
{'sape': 4139, 'jack': 4098,'hena',4087 'guido': 4127}
dict comprehensions can be used to create dictionaries from arbitrary key and value expressions like:
>>> {x: x**2 for x in (2, 4, 6)}
{2: 4, 4: 16, 6: 36}
When the keys are simple strings, it is easier to specify pairs using keyword arguments:
>>>
>>> dict(sape=4139, guido=4127, jack=4098)
{'sape': 4139, 'jack': 4098, 'guido': 4127}

1.11 Date & Time

Date and time can be handled in Python in several ways. Converting between date formats is required in many applications. Python's time and calendar modules help to manipulate dates and times.

Time intervals are floating point numbers in units of seconds. **time** module provides functions for manipulating with times, and for converting between representations. The function *time.time()* returns the current system time in ticks since 12:00am, January 1, 1970(epoch).

Example
        #!/usr/bin/python
        import time; # include time module.
        tick = time.time()
        print ("Number of ticks since 12:00am, January 1, 1970", tick)
        This would produce a result as follows –
        Number of ticks since 12:00am, January 1, 1970: 7186862.73399

1.11.1 TimeTuple

Python's time functions handle time as a tuple of given below 9 numbers –

Index	Field	Values
0	4-digit year	2008
1	Month	1 to 12
2	Day	1 to 31
3	Hour	0 to 23
4	Minute	0 to 59

[Python for Data Analysis]

5	Second	0 to 61 (60 or 61 are leap-seconds)
6	Day of Week	0 to 6 (0 is Monday)
7	Day of year	1 to 366 (Julian day)
8	Daylight savings	-1, 0, 1, -1(library determines DST)

The above tuple is equivalent to **struct_time** structure. This structure has following attributes –

Index	Attributes	Values
0	tm_year	2008
1	tm_mon	1 to 12
2	tm_mday	1 to 31
3	tm_hour	0 to 23
4	tm_min	0 to 59
5	tm_sec	0 to 61 (60 or 61 are leap-seconds)
6	tm_wday	0 to 6 (0 is Monday)
7	tm_yday	1 to 366 (Julian day)
8	tm_isdst	-1, 0, 1, -1 (library determines DST)

1.11.2 Getting current time

Localtime() function returns a time-tuple with all nine items valid.
```
#!/usr/bin/python
import time;
localtime = time.localtime(time.time())
print "Local current time :", localtime
```
Output: –
Local current time : time.struct_time(tm_year=2014, tm_mon=7, tm_mday=17, tm_hour=21, tm_min=26, tm_sec=3, tm_wday=2, tm_yday=195, tm_isdst=0)

1.11.3 Getting formatted time

To get time in readable format is asctime() –
```
#!/usr/bin/python
import time;
localtime = time.asctime( time.localtime(time.time()) )
print "Local current time :", localtime
```
This would produce the following result –
Local current time : Tue Jan 13 10:17:09 2009

1.11.4 Getting calendar for a month

The calendar module gives a wide range of methods to manipulate with yearly and monthly calendars. Here, we print a calendar for a given month (Jan 2009)

```
#!/usr/bin/python
import calendar
cal = calendar.month(2009, 1)
print "Here is the calendar:"
print cal
```

This would produce the following result –

```
Here is the calendar:
January 2009
Mo Tu We Th Fr Sa Su
          1  2  3  4
 5  6  7  8  9 10 11
12 13 14 15 16 17 18
19 20 21 22 23 24 25
26 27 28 29 30 31
```

1.12 How to write Python programs

Example: Using Variables And Literal Constants
Type and run the following program in Python editor:

```
# Filename : var.py
i = 6
print(i)
i = i + 1
print(i)
s = '''This is a multi-line string.
This is the second line.'''
print(s)
```

Run the program
Output:
```
6
7
This is a multi-line string.
This is the second line.
```

1.12.1 Logical and Physical Line

[Python for Data Analysis] 19

A physical line is user *see* when user write the program. A logical line is what *Python sees* as a single statement. Python default assumes that each *physical line* corresponds to a *logical line*.

An example of a logical line is a statement like print ('hello world') if this was on a line by itself , then this also corresponds to a physical line.

Implicitly, Python encourages the use of a single statement per line to makes code more readable.

If you want to write more than one logical line on a single physical line, then you have to explicitly specify this using a semicolon (;) For example:

i = 5
print(i)
is effectively same as
i = 5; print(i)

If it is not possible to write logical single statement in one physical line then *explicit line joining \ is used*:

s = 'This is a string. \
This continues the string.'
print(s)
Output:
This is a string. This continues the string.
Similarly,
i = \
5
is the same as
i = 5

1.12.2 Indentation

Whitespace at the beginning of the line in Python is important. This is called *indentation*. Leading whitespace at the beginning of the logical line is the indentation level of the logical line. This means that statements which go together *should* have the same indentation. Wrong indentation can give rise to errors. For example:

i = 6
# Error below! Due to a single space at the start of the line
 print('Value is', i)
print('I repeat, value is', i)

When you run this, you will get the following error:
  File "whitespace.py", line 3
    print('Value is', i)
    ^
IndentationError: unexpected indent

Chapter 2: Functions, Packages & Classes

2.1 Functions

Function is commonly used to group a series of statements together to perform a logical task.

To declare a function:
>
> def addition(x):
> '''
> This function takes a number as argument and increment the number by 1
> '''
> Print(x+1)

To invoke a function:
>
> >>> addition(5)
> 6
> >>>addition(2)
> 3

return statement

By default, functions return *None*. Function that returns value is called as fruitful function.

>
> def addition(x);
> '''
> This function takes a number as argument and increment the number by 1
> '''
> return x+1

It is a good practice to assign the value to be returned by a function to a variable.
>
> >>>x=addition(5)
> >>>print x
> 6

2.2 Built-in Functions

The python installation is pre-packaged with many modules which contain built in modules. To use a built in module, you have to use the *import* statement.
>
> >>>import math
> >>>math.sqrt(9.0)
> 3
> >>>import random
> >>>random.randint(0,80)
> >>>20

```
>>> def fibon(n):    # write Fibonacci series 0 to n
    """Print a Fibonacci series 0 to n."""
    a, b = 0, 1
    while a < n:
        print(a, end=' ')
        a, b = b, a+b
    print()

>>> # Now call the function
... fib(1000)
0 ,1 , 1 , 2 ,3 , 5 ,8 ,13 ,21 ,34 , 55 ,89 ,144 , 233 ,377 ,610 ,987
```

The keyword *def* is for function *definition*. It must be followed by the function name and list of formal parameters. After this body of the function start, and must be indented.

The *body* of a function store the value in the local symbol table. Variable references first search in following order
1. local symbol table
2. local symbol tables of enclosing functions
3. global symbol table
4. table of built-in names.

Thus global variables cannot be directly assigned a value within a function without a global keyword, but they may be referenced.

The actual parameters to a function call introduce the local symbol table to function; thus, arguments are passed using *call by value*. Whenever a function is called, a new local symbol table is created for every call.

A function definition writes the function name in the current symbol table. The value of the function name recognized as a user-defined function. Thus value can be assigned to another name which can then also be used as a function. This is used as a general renaming mechanism:

```
>>> fib
<function fib at 10041ed0>
>>> f = fib
>>> f(100)
0 ,1 ,1 ,2 ,3 ,5 ,8 ,13, 21 ,34 ,55 ,89
```

You might notice that fib is not a function but it is a procedure because it doesn't return a value. Even the functions which are not having return statement do return a value. This value is called none.

```
>>> fib(2)
>>> print(fib(2))
None
```

[Python for Data Analysis]

Now we are writing a function that returns a list of the numbers of the Fibonacci series, instead of printing with in it:

```
>>> def fibo2(n):  # function returns Fibonacci series from  0 to n
...     """Return Fibonacci series 0 to n."""
...     resultf = []
...     a, b = 0, 1
...     while a < n:
...         resultf.append(a)    # see below
...         a, b = b, a+b
...     return resultf
...
>>> f50 = fib2(50)   # call it
>>> f50              # write the result
[0, 1, 1, 2, 3, 5, 8, 13, 21, 34]
```

The above example demonstrates the followings:
- return statement without an expression argument returns None.
- The method append() adds a new element at the end of the list and equivalent to result = result + [a], but more efficient

2.3 Function Arguments

It is also possible to define functions with a variable number of arguments. There are three forms
1. Default argument values
2. Keyword Arguments
3. Arbitrary Argument List

2.3.1. Default Argument Values

The form is used to specify a default values for arguments. It can create a function that can be called with fewer arguments than it is defined. For example:

```
def ask_for(prompti, retries=4, remind=' try again!'):
    while True:
        ok = input(prompti)
        if ok in ('y', 'yes'):
            return True
        if ok in ('n', 'no', ):
            return False
        retry = retry - 1
        if retry < 0:
            raise ValueError('invalid user response')
```

         print(remind)
Above function can be called in several ways:
- giving only the mandatory arguments: ask_for('Do you want to quit?')
- giving one of the optional arguments: ask_for('OK overwrite the file?', 2)
- or even giving all arguments: ask_for('OK overwrite the file?', 2, ' only yes or no!')

Keyword **in** tests whether or not a sequence contains a certain value.
The default values are evaluated once at the point of function definition in the *defining* scope,
    i = 6
    def f(arg=i):
        print(arg)

    i = 7
    f()
    will print 6.

2.3.2 Keyword Arguments

Keyword arguments are arguments mandatory to be given values at the time of function call.

    def parrotf(voltage, state='maharashtra', action='hit', type='Blue'):
        print("This parrot wouldnot", action, end=' ')
        print("if you put", voltage, "volts through it.")
        print("Lovely plumage, the", type)
        print("-- It's", state, "!")

Functions can be called using keyword arguments with assigned values accepts one required argument (voltage) and three optional arguments (state, action, and type). This function can be called in any of the following ways:

    parrot(1000)   # 1 positional argument
    parrot(voltage=1000)   # one keyword argument
    parrot(voltage=1000000, action='VOOOOM') # two keyword arguments
    parrot(action='VOOOOM', voltage=100000)   # two keyword arguments
    parrot('a million', 'bereft of life', 'jump')   # three positional arguments
    parrot('thousand', state='rajasthans')   # one positional, one keyword
    but all the following calls would be invalid:
    parrot()   # required voltage argument missing

[Python for Data Analysis]

parrot(110, voltage=220)   # duplicate value for the same argument

Note the following points
1. Keyword arguments must follow positional arguments in a function call.
2. All the keyword arguments passed must match one of the arguments accepted by the function and their order is not important.

2.3.3. Arbitrary Argument Lists

A function can be called with an arbitrary number of arguments wrapped in tuples or sequences.

```
def write_multiple_item(file, separator, *args):
    file.write(separator.join(args))  # Join all arguments
```

Any formal parameters which occur after the *args parameter are 'keyword-only' arguments, meaning that they can only be used as keywords (mandatory to provide values at the time of function call) rather than positional arguments.

```
>>> def concat(*args, sep="/"):
...     return sep.join(args)
...
>>> concat("india", "japan", "canada")
'india/japan/canada'
>>> concat("india", "japan", "canada", sep=".")
'india.japan.canada'
```

When a formal parameter of the form **args is present, a dictionary containing all keyword arguments is passed in function call. This may be combined with a formal parameter of the form *name as discussed in previous example.

```
def goodshop(kind, *argument, **keyword):
    print("Do you have any", kind of goods, "?")
    print(" I'm sorry, we are all out of", kind)
    for args in argument:
        print(args)
    print("-" * 40)
    for kws in keyword:
        print(kws, ":", keyword[kw])
```

Function can be called like this:

```
goodshop("soap", "It's fast moving product, sir.",
        "It's really very fast moving product, sir.",
        shopkeeper="Sai",
        client="Ram",
        sketch=" Shop Sketching")
```

Output:
Do you have any soap ?
I'm sorry, we are all out of soap

It's fast moving product, sir.
It's really very fast moving product, sir.
\-
shopkeeper : Sai
client : Ram
sketch : Shop Sketching

2.3.4. Unpacking Argument Lists

Arguments are already in a list or tuple and need to be unpacked during function call for separately processing of individual arguments in list or tuple . It can be done with the built-in range() function with separate *start* and *stop* arguments. If they are not available, with the * operator is used to unpack the arguments out of a list or tuple:

```
>>> list(range(3, 7))        # normal call with start and end
[3, 4, 5,6]
>>> args = [3, 7]
>>> list(range(*args))       # call with * operator to unpacked from a list
[3, 4, 5,6]
```
In the same fashion, dictionaries can be unpacked with **-operator:
```
>>> def parrot(voltage, state1='Unconscious', action1='hit'):
...     print("This bird wouldn't", action, end=' ')
...     print("if you apply", voltage, "volts through it.", end=' ')
...     print("E's", state, "!")
...
>>> d = {"voltage": "five million", "state1": "become unconscious", "action": "HIT"}
>>> parrot(**d)
```
Output: This bird wouldn't HIT if you apply five million volts through it. E's become unconcious !

2.4 Lambda Expressions

Small anonymous functions (function without name) can be created with the lambda keyword.
Given below function returns the increment of argument by n: lambda x:x+n. Lambda functions returns function objects and are restricted to a single expression. Lambda functions can reference only local variable like other functions.
```
>>>
>>> def make_increment(n):
...     return lambda y: y + n
```

```
...
>>> f = make_increment(43)
>>> f(0)
43
>>> f(1)
44
```

Above lambda expression to return a function object. Small function can also be passed as an argument:

```
>>> pair = [(11, 'eleven'), (12, 'twelve'), (13, 'thrirteen'), (14, 'fourteen')]
>>> pair.sort(keys=lambda pair: pair[1])
>>> pair
[(14, 'fourteen'), (11, 'eleven'), (13, 'thirteen'), (12, 'twelve')]
```

2.5. Regular Expressions

Standard python library re supports regular expressions w,hich is bundled with every Python installation. Although library is not PCRE compatible, it supports the majority of common use cases for regular expressions.

2.5.1 Raw Python Strings

When working with regular expression in Python, raw strings can be directly used instead of regular Python strings. Raw strings beginning with r direct interpreter to not to interpret backslashes and special meta characters in the string as they are not regular expression.

This means that a pattern like in raw string "\y\x" will not be interpreted and need not to write this as d of "\\x\\y" as in other languages.

2.5.2 Matching a String

The re package has a methods and classes for string operations like searching, replace etc. Method re.search() returns match object a re.MatchObject with additional information about which part of the string the match was found . And returns None if the pattern doesn't match.
re.search() method stops after the first match.

Method
matchObj= re.search(pattern, input_str, flags=0)

```
import re
# Sub string search using regular expression
```

```
regex1 = r"([a-zA-Z]+) (\d+)"   #value on regex1 is '([a-zA-Z]+) (\\d+)'
if re.search(regex1, "July 25"):
    # The expression "([a-zA-Z]+) (\d+)" matches the date string or we
    can use the MatchObj's start() and end() methods to retrieve substring
    from the input string, and the group() method is used to get all the
    matches in groups.

    match = re.search(regex1, "July 25")

    # This will print Match at index %s, %s 0 7
    print ("string matches at index %s, %s" ,match.start(), match.end())

    # it will print "july 25"
    print ("Matches at %s" , match.group(0))

    # it will print "July"
    print ("Matches at %s" , match.group(1))

    #this will print 25"
    print( "day: %s" , match.group(2))
else:
    # None is returned, does not match
    print ("The regex pattern does not match. :")
```

2.5.3 Capturing Groups

re.findall() to perform a global search and return a list of matches over the whole input string or an empty list if no matches are found.
If you need additional context like starting and ending locations for each match, you can use re.finditer() which returns an iterator of re.MatchObjects to walk through. Although both methods take the same parameters, retrieve same strings but context is not available in findall().

Method
matchlist = re.findall(pattern, input_string, flag=0)
matchlist = re.finditer(pattern, input_string, flag=0)

Example:
```
import re
# regular expression to extract date strings.
regx = r"[a-zA-Z]+ \d+"
matches = re.findall(regx, "July 24, September 9, December 12")
```

[Python for Data Analysis]   29

```
for match in matches:
    print( "Match String: %s" ,(match))
```

This will print:
July 24
September 9
December 12

```
# extract the exact positions of each match
regex = r"([a-zA-Z]+) \d+"
matches = re.finditer(regex, "June 24, August 9, December 12")
for match in matches:
    print ("Match at start end : %s, %s" , match.start(), match.end())
```

Output
    Match at start end *0 7*
    Match at start end *9 17*
    Match at start end *19 29*

2.5.4 Finding and Replacing String

To find and replace a part of a string using regular expressions, method re.sub() can be used. Other arguments like count is the number of replacements in the input string, and this value is less than or equal to zero, then every match in the string is replaced.
replacedstr = re.sub(pattern, replace_pattern, inputstring, count, flags=0)
Example
```
import re
# reverse the order of the day and month in a date string.
regex = r"([a-zA-Z]+) (\d+)"
print (re.sub(regex, r"\2 of \1", "June 24, August 9, December 12"))
```
Output:
24 of June
9 of August
12 of December

2.6 Compiling a Pattern

Sometimes pattern need to be compiled for fast processing and extracting information using the same expression. This method returns a regular expression object.
regxObject = re.compile(pattern, flags=0)

```
import re
# Lets create a pattern and extract some information with it . Pattern is
One or more word then My in a string
regx = re.compile(r"(\w+) My")
result1 = regx.search("Love My Country")
if result1:
    print (result1.start(), result1.end())
    Output will be
    0  7 for the start and end of the match

for result1 in regx.findall("Right My, Left My"):
    print( result1)
```

Output:
Right
Left

2.7 Classes & Objects

Python is object oriented language. Like any other object oriented language C++/JAVA programmer can create classes and objects and all object oriented language features are applicable.

2.7.1 Creating Classes

Class statement is used to create a new class. It is used for class definition.

```
class Student:
    'student class and its methods'
    stCount = 0

    def __init__(self, name, age):
        self.name = name
        self.age = age
        Student.stCount += 1

    def totalCount(self):
        print ("Total Students %d" , Student.stCount)

    def displaystudent(self):
        print ("Name : ", self.name, ", Age ", self.age)
```

The variable declared before any method (starting of class) stCount is a class variable accessible to all instances of a this class. This can be accessed as Student.stCount from inside the class or outside the class.

The class constructor is written using method __init__(). When you create a new instance of this class, this method is automatically called.

Other class methods are defined like normal methods with the exception that the first argument to every method is self. When you call these methods, you need not to include as self.

2.7.2 Object & Instance Variable

Object of a class can be created by calling class using class name and pass required parameters as in its __init__ method definition.

    " create first object of Student class"
    St1 = Student("Jayesh", 16)
    " create second object of student class"
    St22 = Student("Manali", 17)

Instance variables are owned by instances of the class. This means that for each object or instance of a class, the instance variables are different. Unlike class variables, instance variables are defined within methods.

In the Shark class example below, name and age are instance variables:

    class Shark:
      def __init__(self, name, age):
        self.name = name
        self.age = age

2.7.3 Accessing Attributes

Attributed of an objects can be accessed using dot(.) operator. Class variable can accessed using class name.variable as given below.

    st1.displaystudent()
    st2.displaystudent()
    print("Total Students %d" % Student.stCount)

In all when above program is executed output will be

    Name : Jayesh ,Age: 16
    Name : Manali ,Age: 17
    Total Students 2

You can add, delete, or update attributes of classes and objects –

st1.branch = "Computer"   # Add 'branch' attribute.
St1.branch = "Electrical"   # Modify 'branch' attribute.
del st.branch   # Delete 'branch' attribute.

Inbuilt functions can be directly used to access attributes −
The getattr(object, name[, default]) : to access an attribute of the object.
The hasattr(object,name) : to check if an attribute exists then return true.
The setattr(object,name,value) : to set value of an attribute. If attribute does not exist, then it is created.
The delattr(object, name) : to delete an attribute.
hasattr(st1, 'branch')   # Returns true if 'branch' attribute exists
getattr(st1, 'branch')   # Returns value of 'branch' attribute
setattr(st1, 'age', 15) # Set attribute 'age' at 15
delattr(stl, 'age')   # Delete attribute 'age'

2.7.4 Built-In Class Attributes

Python support built-in attributes to access class name, base class name, module names, class dictionary etc.
  dict : Dictionary containing the class's namespace.
  __doc__ : Class documentation if defined it returns string or none.
  __name__ : Class name.
  __module__ : Module name in which the class is defined.
  __bases__ : A possibly empty tuple containing the base classes, in the order of their occurrence in the base class list.

2.7.5 Creating Constructor

A constructor is a special kind of method that Python calls when it instantiates an object using the definitions found in your class. Python relies on the constructor to perform tasks such as initializing (assigning values to) any instance variables that the object will need when it starts. Constructors can also verify that there are enough resources for the object and perform any other start-up task you can think of.

The name of a constructor is always the same, __init__(). The constructor can accept arguments when necessary to create the object. When you create a class without a constructor, Python automatically creates a default constructor for you that doesn't do anything. Every class must have a constructor, even if it simply relies on the default constructor.

For the above class let us try to access all these attributes given above −

#!/usr/bin/python

```
class Student:
   ' Base class for all students'
   stCount = 0

   def __init__(self, name, age):
     self.name = name
     self.age = age
     Student.stCount += 1

   def totalCount(self):
     print ("Total Students %d" , Student.stCount)

   def displayStudent(self):
     print ("Student Name : ", self.name, ", Age: ", self.age)

print ("Student.__doc__:", Student.__doc__)
print ("Student.__name__:", Student.__name__)
print ("Student.__module__:", Student.__module__)
print ("Student.__bases__:", Student.__bases__)
print ("Student.__dict__:", Student.__dict__)
```

When the code is executed, it produces the following result −

Student.__doc__: Base class for all students
Student.__name__: Student
Student.__module__: __main__
Student.__bases__: (<class 'object'>,)
Student.__dict__: {'__module__': '__main__', '__doc__': ' Base class for all students', 'stCount': 0, '__init__': <function Student.__init__ at 0x02ADC858>, 'totalCount': <function Student.totalCount at 0x02F13348>, 'displayStudent': <function Student.displayStudent at 0x03394D20>, '__dict__': <attribute '__dict__' of 'Student' objects>, '__weakref__': <attribute '__weakref__' of 'Student' objects>}
>>>

2.8 Destroying Objects

Python deletes unwanted objects automatically to free the memory space . The process by which Python periodically reclaims blocks of memory which are no longer in use is termed Garbage Collection.

Python's garbage collector is automatically executed during program execution and whenever object's reference count reaches zero ,it is triggered . An object's reference count zero means no aliases points to it.

When new object is created object's reference count is 1. When it is assigned a new name or placed in a container (list, tuple, or dictionary) it's reference count increases. The object's reference count decreases when either it's deleted with del or its reference is reassigned. When an object's reference count reaches zero garbage collector automatically starts.

```
x = 30     # Create object <30>
y = x      # Increase reference count by 1 of <30>
z = [y]    # Increase reference count by 1 of <30>

del x      # Decrease reference count by 1 of <30>
y = 100    # Decrease reference count by 1 of <30>
z[0] = -1  # Decrease reference count by 1 of <30>
```

A class can implement the a destructor __del__(), explicitly , which is invoked when the instance is about to be destroyed.

Example
This __del__() destructor is user defined which prints the class name of an instance that is about to be destroyed

```
#!/usr/bin/python

class Scale:
  def __init( self, a=0, b=0):
    self.a = a
    self.b = b
  def __del__(self):
    class_name = self.__class__.__name__
    print ( class_name, "destroyed")

sc1 = Point()
sc2 = sc1
sc3 = sc1
print (id(sc1), id(sc2), id(sc3) )

del sc1
del sc2
del sc3
```

[Python for Data Analysis]   35

When the above code is executed, it produces following result –

10595568 10595568 10595568
Scale destroyed

2.9 Class Inheritance

Instead of writing new class , you can create a class by deriving it from a pre existing class. Child class can inherit features of base class and additional required features can be added . It can be written as child class name(base class name) .

A child class can also override attributes and methods from the parent class.

```
class Parentclass:        # define parent class
   pAttribute = 100
   def __init__(self):
      print ("Parent constructor")

   def pMethod(self):
      print ('Parent method definition')

   def setAttr(self, attrib):
      Parentclass. pAttribute = attrib

   def getAttr(self):
      print ("Get attribute in parent class :", Parentclass. pAttribute)

class Child(Parentclass):  # define child class
   def __init__(self):
      print (" child constructor")

   def childMethod(self):
      print ('Defining child method')

cc = Child()        # instance of child
```

```
cc.childMethod()    # child method call
cc.pMethod()    # parent method call
cc.setAttr(200)    # set attributes in parent's method
cc.getAttr()    # get attributes in parent's method
```

When the above code is executed, it produces the following result –

child constructor
Defining child method
Parent method definition
Get attribute in parent class : 200

Mutiple Inheritance: you can drive a class from multiple parent classes.

```
class A:    # Base class A
class B:    # Base class B
.....

class C(A, B):   #  C inherits (subclass of) class A and B
.....
```

To check subclass or relationship in classes and instances issubclass() or isinstance() methods can be used.
The issubclass(subclassname, superclassname) boolean function returns true if the subclassname is indeed a subclass of the superclassname.
The is instance(obj, Class) boolean function returns true if obj is an instance of class or is an instance of a its subclass.

2.10 Overriding Methods

Override methods are the methods with same signature redefined in subclass. Reason for overriding parent's methods is that we may want different functionality to be defined in subclass.

Example
```
#!/usr/bin/python

class Base:    # defining base class
  def baseMethod(self):
    print('Base Module')

class Child(Base): # defining subclass of base class
  def baseMethod (self):
```

```
        print('Child module')
c = Child()         # instance of subclass
c.baseMethod()      #  overridden method in child is called
```

When the above code is executed, it produces the following result −

Child module

2.10.1 Base Overloading Methods

Following table lists some generic functionality built in methods that you can override in your own classes

SN	Method,	Description
1	__init__ (self [,args...])	Constructor
2	__del__ (self)	Delete the object
3	__repr__ (self)	Represent the string (evaluatable)
4	__str__ (self)	String Processing
5	__cmp__ (self, x)	Object Comparison

Overloading Operators

Overloading operators is to keep method name same in base and child class but parameters are different.Suppose you have + method to add two vectors or two complex numbers.
You could, however, overload the __add__ method in your class to perform vector addition as given below..

```
class Vectoraddition:
    def __init__(self, x, y):
        self.x = x
        self.y = y
    def __str__(self):  # convert in integer
        return 'Vector (%d, %d)' % (self.x, self.y)
    def __add__(self,other):
        return Vectoraddition(self.x + other.x, self.y + other.y)
v1 = Vectoraddition(2,10)
v2 = Vectoraddition(5,-2)
print (v1 + v2)
```

Output

Vector(7,8)

2.10.2 Data Hiding

If an object's attributes is visible only within class but is not visible through object.attribute outside the class definition. You need to define name attributes with a double underscore prefix.

```
class createCounter:
   __checkCount = 0

   def count(self):
      self.__checkCount += 1
      print (self.__checkCount)

counterobj = createCounter()
counterobj.count()
counterobj.count()
print (counterobj.__createCount)
```

Output:

1
2
Traceback (most recent call last):
  File "C:\Users\HP\AppData\Local\Programs\Python\Python36-32\nu.py", line 11, in <module>
    print (counterobj.__createCount)
AttributeError: 'createCounter' object has no attribute '__createCount'

If you access same attribute like object._className__attrName, you can access it outside class too. If you replace last line in above code by
print (counterobj._createCounter__checkCount)

Output:
1
2
2

2.11 Exception Handling

Errors that occur at run time are raised as exception by Python. Syntactically correct statements can also cause error at run time like divide by zero. Most of the exceptions are not handled by programs and result in error messages as given below:

>>> 9 * (1/0)
Traceback (most recent call last):
 File "<pyshell#1>", line 1, in <module>
   9 * (1/0)
ZeroDivisionError: division by zero

>>> '1' + 1
Traceback (most recent call last):
 File "<pyshell#2>", line 1, in <module>
   '1' + 1
TypeError: must be str, not int

The last line of the error message indicates type of error. Exceptions types can be ZeroDivisionError, NameError and TypeError. Exception message contains exception type (name of the built-in exception) that occurred. Exception types printed in message are built in exception for few standard exceptions but exceptions can also be user defined.

In addition to exception name , the context where the exception happened , line number (a stack traceback listing source lines) and other related details are also displayed.

2.11.1 . Handling Exceptions

Exceptions can be handled in selected cases. Given below is program ask user to input a valid integer but when user interrupt the program either using Control-C C or whatever the operating system supports or user input alphabet rather than number. User generated interrupt KeyboardInterrupt exception is raised and handled.

```
while True:
    try:
        x = int(input("Enter a number: "))
        break
    except ValueError:
        print("It is not a valid number.  Try again...")
```

Output:

Enter a number: a
It is not a valid number. Try again...

The try statement works as follows.

First, the try clause is executed (Statements under try).
If exception is not found exception clause will not be executed.
If exception is found in try clause, except clause is immediately executed ,rest of instruction in try clause are skipped .
If exception occurs does not match the type of exception handling, control passed on to outer try clause. If no handler is found, unhandled exception message is displayed.
If an exception occurs which does not match the exception handled in the except clause, control is passed on to outer try statements; if no handler is found, it is an unhandled exception and execution stops with a message by system.

A try statement may have more than one handler for different exceptions. At most one related handler corresponding to try clause will be executed. An except clause may have multiple exceptions name as a parenthesized tuple given below:

   except (RuntimeError, TypeError, NameError):

2.11.2. Raising Exceptions

Programmer can raise an exception to force a specified exception. For example:

\>>>raise NameError('Hi')
Traceback (most recent call last):
  File "\<pyshell#4>", line 1, in \<module>
    raise NameError('Hi')
  NameError: Hi

The argument to raise is exception name to be raised. This must be either an exception instance or an exception class. If an exception class is passed, it's constructor will be automatically executed.

raise ValueError # In place of 'raise ValueError()'
Traceback (most recent call last):
  File "\<pyshell#5>", line 1, in \<module>
    raise ValueError
ValueError

[Python for Data Analysis]

2.12 Modules

A module allows us to organize logically related python code at one place. This makes code easier to understand and use. A module is a Python object that bind variables, functions and classes together for reference.
Example
The Python code for a module named mypack normally saved as mypack.py.
Example: mypack.py

```
def print_func( par ):
    print "Hello : ", par
    return
```

2.12.1 The import Statement

You can use already defined Python module by using an import statement in some other Python source file. The import has the following syntax:
import module1[, module2[,... moduleN]
When an import statement encounter, it imports the module. The module is searched in the search path as described in section given below. A search path is a list of directories where the interpreter searches when importing a module.

```
#!/usr/bin/python

# Import module mypack
import mypack

# Call function of mypack
mypack.print_func("Zara")
```

When the above code is executed, it produces the following result –
Hello : Zara
A module is loaded only once even if multiple imports occur. This prevents the module execution happening again and again.

The from...import Statement
Python's from statement allow you import specific attribute or function from a module into the current namespace. The from...import has the following syntax –
from modulename import name1[, name2[, ... nameN]]
For example, to import the function Fibonacci from the module fibpack, use the following statement –

from fibpack import Fibonacci

This statement import just fibonacci from the module fibpack into the current namespace. Instead of entire module fibpack.

The from...import * Statement:
To import all names from a module into the current namespace by using given below statement –

from modulename import *

2.12.2 Locating Modules

When import statement is executed, Python searches modules in following sequences:-

1. First module will be searched in current directory.
2. Then searches each path in the shell variable PYTHONPATH.
3. After this Python checks in default path.

This module search path is stored in the system module sys as the sys.path variable. The sys.path variable contains the current directory, PYTHONPATH, default path.

The PYTHONPATH Variable:

The PYTHONPATH is an environment variable, whose value is set as list of directories. This is the path where the module is searched. To set value in PYTHONPATH in a Windows system:

set PYTHONPATH=c:\python20\lib;

To set value in PYTHONPATH in a LINUX system

set PYTHONPATH=/usr/local/lib/python

2.13. Packages

A package is a single application environment consists of modules, sub packages etc. It is a hierarchical directory structure .
Consider a file mymodule.py available in mydirectory directory. This file has following line of code –

```python
#!/usr/bin/python

def modu():
    print("mymodule")
    return
```

Now, create one more file __init__.py in mydirectory directory –

mydirectory/__init__.py

To make all of your functions available when you've imported modu, you need to put explicit import statements in __init__.py as follows –

from mydirectory.mymodule import modu

After you add these lines to __init__.py,

Create test.py file in to check package availability. You have to make all these classes available when you import the mydirectory package.

```python
#!/usr/bin/python

import mydirectory
def t():
    mydirectory.modu()
t()
```

Output:mymodule

In the above example, we have taken an example of a single functions in one file, but you can keep multiple functions in your files. You can also define different Python classes in those files and then you can create your packages out of those classes.

CHAPTER 3: NUMPY & MATPLOTLIB

3.1 Arrays

Python doesn't have a array data structure but have list which is more generalised and can be used as multidimensional array.

List basics

A list is an ordered collection of items of different type. List is more flexible than array but difficult to handle when it works with regular structure. Array is an ordered collection of items of a single type and works well with regular structure. A list is a dynamic mutable type and this means you can add and delete elements from the list at any time in contrast to static data type array..
To define a list you have to write a comma separated items enclosed in square brackets:
      myItems=[1,2,3,4,5,6]
To pick an element from an array, "slicing" notation is used. Like array index start from 0 and index 3 is fourth element in list.
      print myItems[3]
      Output:4
Similarly to change the fourth element, direct value can be assigned.
      myItems[3]=100

The slicing notation extract sublist from starting to ending locations specified in index as given below .
　　　myItems[2:5]
　　　Output:
　　　[3,4,5]
Elements will be extracted from myItems[2] to myItems[4] , final element specified i.e. [5] is not included in the slice.Either of the start or end indexes can be left out and they will be assumed to have their start or end index of list depends on first or later part is left. For example
myItem[4:]
is the list from List[4] to the end of the list and
myItem[:4]
is the list from start up to myItem[4] and
myItem[:]entire list.
List slicing can be modified by assignment. For example:
myItem[0:2]=[1,2]
has the same effect as
myItem[0]=1
myItem[1]=2
To assign to a slice need not to have the same size as the slice - it simply replaces it even if it is of different size.To do list operations, list is to be scanned :
　　　m=0
　　　for ele in myItem:
　　　 if m<ele:
　　　　m=ele
　　　#This uses the for..in construct to scan through each item in the list.
　　　Alternatively list can be scanned #through indexing.
　　　Item=0
　　　for i in range(len(myItem)):
　　　 if Item<myItem[i]:
　　　　Item=myItem[i]
Range is used to generate the sequence 0,1,.. end index and all items in list are sequentially scanned.For example if you wanted to return not the maximum element but its index position in the list you could use:
　　　m=0
　　　mi=0
　　　for i in range(len(myItem)):
　　　 if m<myItem[i]:
　　　　m=myItem[i]
　　　　mi=i
or you could use the non-indexed loop and the index method:
　　　m=0

```
for e in myItem:
 if m<e:
  m=e
mi=myItem.index(m)
print mi
```

3.2 Numpy

Numpy is a numerical computation engine, to perform scientific computations.

3.2.1 Getting Numpy

The standard Python package manager is called *pip*.pip is used to install some additional packages which are not part of standard python. You have to run following on command prompt. Change current directory as where python is installed and run command like

C:/program files/python35/scripts/pip> pip install numpy

To check that numpy is installed properly or not. On Python script check

```
File Edit Shell Debug Options Window Help
Python 3.6.0 (v3.6.0:41df79263a11, Dec 23 2016, 07:18:10) [MSC v.1900 32 bit (Intel)]
Type "copyright", "credits" or "license()" for more information.
>>> import numpy
>>>
>>>
```

Type in "import numpy" and press Enter. If Python comes back with another prompt after a second, everything's working correctly.

On Linux

sudo pip install numpy

sudo apt-get install libatlas-base-dev gfortran

sudo pip install scipy

sudo pip install matplotlib

3.2.2 2D Numpy Arrays

NumPy is the fundamental package for scientific computing. It is a N- dimensional array object contains tools capable to integrate with C/C++/ Fortran code. It perform linear algebra, random number capabilities and Fourier transform etc.

NumPy is an efficient multi-dimensional container of generic data. In Big Data , NumPy allow seamlessly and speedily integrate with a arbitrary and variety of data.It is a table of elements usually numbers. NumPy dimensions are called axes. The rank of numpy is number of axis.

For example, in one dimensional array [1, 2, 2] ,has one axis and one rank .That axis has a length of 3.

[Python for Data Analysis]

In the example pictured below, the array has rank 2 (it is 2-dimensional). The first dimension (axis) has a length of 2 (number of rows), the second dimension has a length of 3 (number of columns).

[[1., 0., 1.],
 [0., 2., 2.]]

Python standard library supports array which handles only one-dimensional arrays with less functionality. NumPy's array class is called ndarray. It is also known by the alias array and referred as numpy.array.

The other attributes of an ndarray object are:

ndarray.ndim
> Represents the number of dimensions (axis) of the array. It is also known as rank of an array.

ndarray.shape
> the dimensions of the array. It indicats the size of the array in each dimension. For a N rows and M columns matrix, shape is (n,m). Rank is two and ndim is 2.

ndarray.size
> the total number of elements in an array. Size is equal to n*m in above example i.e. multiplication of dimensions.

ndarray.dtype

displays the type of the elements in the array. Programmer can create or specify dtype's using standard Python types. NumPy provides other types of its own like numpy.int32, numpy.int16, and numpy.float64.

ndarray.itemsize

the size in bytes used by each element of an array. For example, an array of elements of type int32 has itemsize 4 (=32/8). It is equivalent to ndarray.dtype.itemsize.

An example: This creates a numpy array and performs various operations on it.

>>> import numpy as np
>>> x = np.arange(20).reshape(4, 5)
>>> x
array([[0, 1, 2, 3, 4],
       [5, 6, 7, 8, 9],
       [10, 11, 12, 13, 14]]
       [15, 16, 17, 18, 19])
>>> x.shape
(4, 5)
>>> x.ndim
2
>>> x.dtype.name
'int64'
>>> x.itemsize

8
>>> x.size
20

3.2.3 Array Creation

An array can be created by using the array function. The data type of an array is deduced from the type of the elements.
>>> a = np.array([0,1,2,3,4])
>>> a
array([0,1,2, 3, 4])
>>> a.dtype
dtype('int64')
>>> b = np.array([0.5,1.2, 3.5, 5.1])
>>> b.dtype
dtype('float64')

Array list is to be enclosed by square brackets .
Two dimensional arrays can be defined as :-
>>> b = np.array([(1,2,3), (4,5,6)])
>>> b
array([[1, 2 , 3],
   [4 , 5 , 6]])
The type of the array can be specified at creation time also:
>>> c = np.array([[6,7], [8,9]], dtype=complex)
>>> c
array([[6.+0.j, 7.+0.j],
   [8.+0.j, 9.+0.j]])

When the size of array is initially known but elements are not known. We can define the array by using size only. We can also use function which auto fill array along with definition.

np.zeros():Creates an array full of zeros

np.ones():Creates an array full of ones

np.arrange(): Generates an array from starting to end point increased by interval value

By default, the dtype of the created array is float64.
>>> np.zeros((3,3))
array([[0., 0., 0.],
   [0., 0., 0.],
   [0., 0., 0.]])
To generate sequences of numbers
>>> np.arange(10, 20, 5)

[Python for Data Analysis]

array([10, 15, 20])

When arange is used with floating point arguments, number of elements cannot be predicted, due to the finite floating point precision. To overcome this problem the function linspace can be used which receives as an argument the number of elements that we want to generate.

>>> np.linspace(0, 2, 9)   # 9 numbers from 0 to 2
array([0. , 0.25, 0.5 , 0.75, 1. , 1.25, 1.5 , 1.75, 2.])

3.2.4 Printing Arrays

NumPy support multi dimensional array. It can be displayed in a similar way to nested lists, but with the following layout:
- the last axis is printed from left to right,
- the second-to-last axis is printed from top to bottom,
- the rest of axis are also printed from top to bottom, with each slice separated from the next by an empty line.

One-dimensional arrays are printed as single row, bidimensional arrays are as matrices and tridimensional arrays as lists of matrices.

>>> a = np.arange(5)   # 1d array
>>> print(a)
[0 1 2 3 4]
>>> b = np.arange(6).reshape(2,3)   # 2d array
>>> print(b)
[[0 1 2]
 [3 4 5]]

If an array is too large, NumPy prints only corners and skip the other part:
>>>
>>> print(np.arange(1000))
[0   1   2 ..., 999]

3.2.5 Numpy Basic Array Operations

Arithmetic operators are applied ELEMENTWISE and result in a new array.
>>> a = np.array([20,30,40,50])
>>> b = np.array([2,3,3,2])
>>> c = a+b
>>> c
array([22, 33, 43, 52])

Multiply operator (*) in Numpy also operates element wise unlike in other languages. It can be performed using the dot function or method:
>>> A = np.array([[1,1],[0,1]])

```
>>> B = np.array( [[2,0], [3,4]] )
>>> C=A*B              # elementwise product
>>>C
Output:
array([[2, 2],
    [3, 4]])

>>> C=A.dot(B)         # matrix product
>>>C
Output
array([[5, 6],
    [5, 6]])
```

Many unary functions, such as computing the sum of all the elements in the array, are implemented as methods of the ndarray class.

```
>>> A=np.array([1,2,3,4])
>>> A.sum()
10
>>> a.min()
1
>>> a.max()
4
```

In multidimensional arrays unary functions can perform functions axis wise by specifying the axis parameter.

```
>>> b = np.arange(6).reshape(2,3)
>>> b
array([[0, 1, 2],
    [3, 4, 5]])
>>>
>>> b.sum(axis=0)           #Sum of each column
array([3, 5, 7])

>>> b.sum (axis=1)          #Sum of each row
array([ 3, 12])

>>> b.cumsum(axis=1) # cumulative sum along each row
array([[ 0, 1, 3],
    [ 3, 7, 12]], dtype=int32)
```

3.2.6 Universal Functions

NumPy provides familiar mathematical functions such as sin, cos, sqrt, and exp. Within NumPy, these functions operate element wise on an array, producing an array as output.

```
>>> B = np.arange(4)
>>> B
array([0, 1, 2, 3])

>>> np.exp(B)
array([ 1.       ,  2.71828183,  7.3890561 , 20.08553692])

>>> np.sqrt(B)
array([ 0.       ,  1.       ,  1.41421356,  1.73205081])>>> C = np.array([2., -1., 4.])
```

3.2.7 Indexing, Slicing and Iterating

One-dimensional arrays can be indexed, sliced and iterated over to read, access and retrieve elements or its subset.

```
>>> a = np.arange(10)**2
>>> a
array([ 0,  1,  4,  9, 16, 25, 36, 49, 64, 81])
>>> a[3]
9
>>> a[3:5]
array([ 9, 16])
>>> a[:5:2] = -1000    # equivalent to a[0:5:2] = -1000; from start to position 5, exclusive, set every 2nd element to -1000
>>> a
array([-1000,    1, -1000,    9, -1000,   25,   36,   49,   64,   81])
>>> a[::-1]            #reverse a
array([   81,   64,   49,   36,   25, -1000,    9, -1000,    1, -1000])
```

Multidimensional arrays can have one index per axis. These indices are given in a tuple separated by commas:

```
>>> def f(x,y):
...     return x+y

>>> b = np.fromfunction(f,(4,5),dtype=int)
>>> b
array([[0, 1, 2, 3, 4],
       [1, 2, 3, 4, 5],
       [2, 3, 4, 5, 6],
```

```
        [3, 4, 5, 6, 7]])
>>> b[2,3]              #2nd row, 3rd col (start= 0th row)
5
>>> b[0:4,1]            #row 1 display
array([1, 2, 3, 4])
>>> b[ : ,1]            # equivalent to the previous example
array([1, 2, 3, 4])
>>> b[1:3, : ]          #Display all columns from 1st and 2nd row (start=
0th row)
array([[1, 2, 3, 4, 5],
       [2, 3, 4, 5, 6]])
```

3.2.8 Splitting an Array

Function hsplit, can be used to split an array along its horizontal axis, either by specifying the number of equally shaped arrays to return, or by specifying the columns after which the division should occur:

```
>>> a=np.floor(10*np.random.random((2,12)))  #create 2 by 12 array of
random numbers
>>> a
array([[ 9., 8., 4., 8., 8., 4., 1., 2., 6., 8., 0., 1.],
       [ 2., 7., 9., 9., 2., 7., 8., 1., 2., 9., 7., 5.]])

>>> np.hsplit(a,4)   # Split a into 4

[array([[ 9., 8., 4.],
       [ 2., 7., 9.]]), array([[ 8., 8., 4.],
       [ 9., 2., 7.]]), array([[ 1., 2., 6.],
       [ 8., 1., 2.]]), array([[ 8., 0., 1.],
       [ 9., 7., 5.]])]

>>> np.hsplit(a,(2,6))  ))   # Split a after 2nd and the 6th column

[array([[ 9., 8.],
       [ 2., 7.]]), array([[ 4., 8., 8., 4.],
       [ 9., 9., 2., 7.]]), array([[ 1., 2., 6., 8., 0., 1.],
       [ 8., 1., 2., 9., 7., 5.]])]
```
vsplit will splits along the vertical axis in an array in similar way.

3.2.9 Statistical Functions

NumPy has useful functions to perform statistical operations like finding minimum, percentile standard deviation ,maximum and variance, etc. from the given elements in the array. The functions are explained as follows −numpy.amin() and numpy.amax()
These functions return the minimum and the maximum from the elements in the given array along the specified axis.

Example
```
import numpy as np
a = np.array([[1,2,3],[4,5,6],[7,8,9]])

print ('Our array is:' )
print (a)
print ('\n')

print ('amin() on axis 1 to find min in each row' )
print (np.amin(a,1))
print ('\n')

print ('Applying amin() on axis 0:' )
print (np.amin(a,0))
print ('\n')

print ('Applying amax() on overall values ' )
print (np.amax(a))
print ('\n' )

print ('Applying amax() on axis 0' )
print (np.amax(a, axis = 0))
```
It will produce the following output

Our array is:

[[1 2 3]
 [4 5 6]
 [7 8 9]]
amin() on axis 1 to find min in each row
[1 4 7]
Applying amin() on axis 0:
[1 2 3]
Applying amax() on overall values
9
Applying amax() on axis 0
[7 8 9]

numpy.median()

Median is defined as the value separating the higher half from the lower half in a sequence. The numpy.median() function is used to return middle value form a sequence..

Example

```
import numpy as np
a = np.array([[30,40,50],[60,70,80],[90,100,110]])
print ('Our array is:' )
print (a)
print ('Applying median() on all values:')
print (np.median(a))
print ('Applying median() on  axis 0:')
print (np.median(a, axis = 0))
print ('Applying median() on  axis 1:')
print (np.median(a, axis = 1))
```

It will produce the following output –

Our array is:

[[30 40 50]
 [60 70 80]
 [90 100 110]]

Applying median() on all values:
70.0
Applying median() on axis 0:
[60. 70. 80.]
Applying median() on axis 1:
[40. 70. 100.]

numpy.mean()

Arithmetic mean = (the sum of elements along an axis)/ (the number of elements)

The numpy.mean() function returns the arithmetic mean of elements in the array. It works in similar way as other statistical functions if axis is given as parameter in function.

numpy.average()

Weighted average is an average of values along the specified axis. It can also calculate weighted average. The numpy.average() function computes the weighted average of elements in an array according to weight given . The function can also have an axis parameter for axis wise calculation.

Standard Deviation

Standard deviation is the square root of the average of squared deviations from mean. The formula for standard deviation is as follows –
std = sqrt(mean(abs(x - x.mean())**2))

Example
import numpy as np
>>> print (np.std([5,5,6,5]))
0.433012701892

Variance

Variance is the average of squared deviations, i.e., mean(abs(y - y.mean())**2). The standard deviation is the square root of variance. Variance depicts the variability in values.

Example
import numpy as np
>>> print (np.var([2,2,4,4]))
1.0

3.3 Matplotlib

3.3.1 Getting Matpolib

Installing Matplotlib on Linux

If you're using the version of Python that came with your system, you can use your system's package manager to install matplotlib. For Python 3, this is:
$ sudo apt-get install python3-matplotlib

If you want to install a newer version of Python, you'll have to install several other libraries that matplotlib depends on:

$ sudo apt-get install python3.5-dev python3.5-tk tk-dev
$ sudo apt-get install libfreetype6-dev g++
Then use pip to install matplotlib:
$ pip install --user matplotlib
Installing matplotlib on Windows

First download matplot library from https://pypi.python.org/pypi/matplotlib/ and look for a wheel file (a file ending in .WHL) that matches the version of

Python you're using. For example,if you're using a 32-bit version of Python 3.5, you'll need to download MATPLOTLIB-1.4.3-CP35-NONE-WIN32.WHL.

Then use pip command on windows command prompt in related python directory to install matplotlib:

pip install matplotlib

3.3.2 Introduction to Matplotlib

Matplotlib in a Python is 2D plotting library which generates quality figures for publication and interactive environments across platforms.

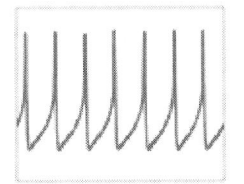

Matplotlib can generate plots, scatterplots,histograms, power spectra, bar charts, errorcharts, etc.,.

For simple plotting the pyplot provides a an interface to the matplotlib object-oriented plotting library. It gives full control of axes properties, line styles, font properties, etc, to the programmer.

3.3.3 Simple Plot

To use functions defined in pyplot , you have to import specific module pyplot of Matplotlib instead of all modules of Matplotlib. This saves memory space.

Matplotlib's modules comes with a set of default settings . Programmer can control the default values of almost every property like color and style ,figure size and dpi, line width, axes, axis and grid properties, text and font properties and so on.

Example: Generate values and calculate its sin() and cos() and plot.

```
import numpy as np
import matplotlib.pyplot as pl
#generate 256 values from -3.14 to +3.14
X = np.linspace(-np.pi, np.pi, 256, endpoint=True)
print(X)
CP = np.cos(X)
SP= np.sin(X)
pl.plot(X,CP)
pl.plot(X,SP)
pl.show()
```

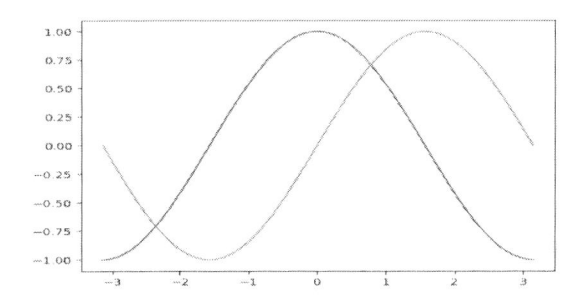

Changing Colors and Line Width

Now we are changing default values defined by Matplotlib in above program. For example we want to have the cosine curve in blue and the sine curve in red and a slightly thicker line for both of them in plot. We also wish to slightly alter the figure size to make it more horizontal.

```
pl.figure(figsize=(10,6), dpi=80)
pl.plot(X, CP, color="blue", linewidth=2.5, linestyle="-")
pl.plot(X, SP, color="red", linewidth=2.5, linestyle="-")
```

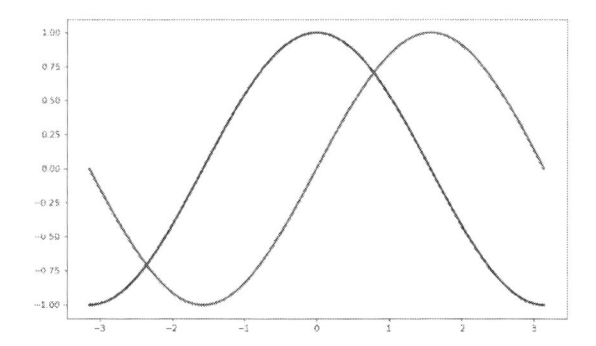

Setting Limits

Current limits of the figure are a bit too tight and we want to make some space in order to clearly see all data points. X axis and Y axis starts from 1.5 and 1.5 of default limits.
pl.xlim(X.min()*1.5, X.max()*1.5)
pl.ylim(CP.min()*1.5, CP.max()*1.5)

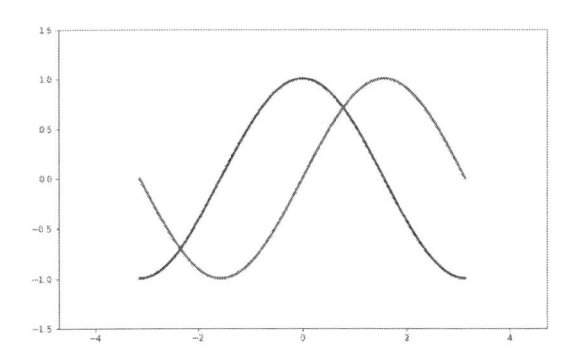

Setting Ticks

Current ticks (Values on X and Y axis) are not ideal because they do not show the values (+/-π,+/-π/2) for sine and cosine. We can change them by using xticks() and yticks().

...
pl.xticks([-np.pi, -np.pi/2, 0, np.pi/2, np.pi])
pl.yticks([-1, 0, +1])
...

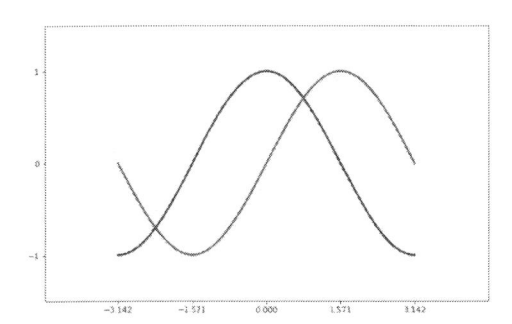

Setting Tick Labels

Ticks proper values are now placed but their label is not very convincing. We wish to place symbols π on plot.

[Python for Data Analysis]

pl.xticks([-np.pi, -np.pi/2, 0, np.pi/2, np.pi], [r'$-\pi$', r'$-\pi/2$', r'0', r'$+\pi/2$', r'$+\pi$'])

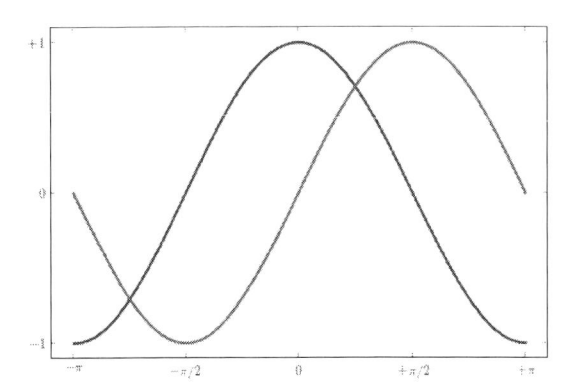

pl.yticks([-1, 0, +1], [r'-1', r'0', r'$+1$'])

...

Moving Spines

Spines are the reference axis lines connecting the tick marks . They can be placed at arbitrary positions ,in previous example they were placed on the border of plot. We can change, bring them in the middle. Since there are four of them (top/bottom/left/right), we can discard the top and right by setting their color to none and will move the bottom and left ones to coordinate 0 in data space coordinates.

axs = pl.gca()
axs.spines['right'].set_color('none')
axs.spines['top'].set_color('none')
axs.xaxis.set_ticks_position('bottom')
axs.spines['bottom'].set_position(('data',0))   #Place x axis on centre
axs.yaxis.set_ticks_position('left')
axs.spines['left'].set_position(('data',0))   #Place y axis on centre

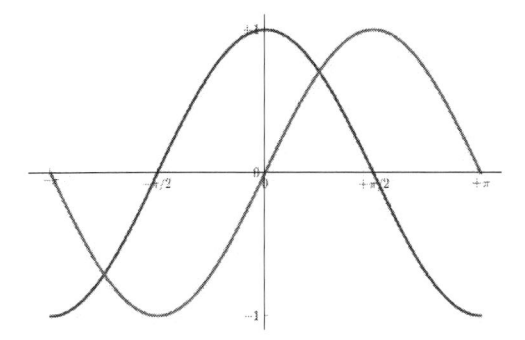

Adding a legend

We can add a legend in the upper left corner. This is required for adding the keyword argument label to the plot commands.
plt.plot(X, CP, color="blue", linewidth=2.5, linestyle="-", label="cosine")
plt.plot(X, SP, color="red", linewidth=2.5, linestyle="-", label="sine")
plt.legend(loc='upper left', frameon=False)

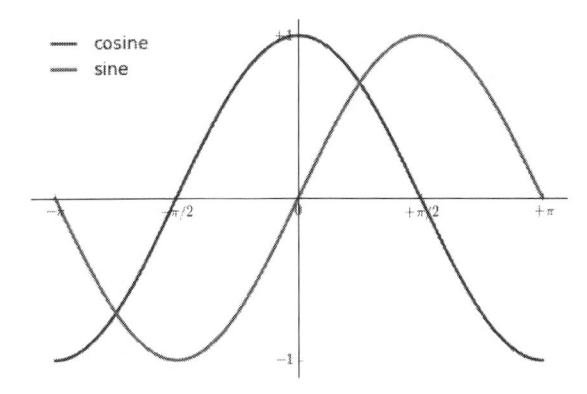

So complete program will be
```
import numpy as np
import matplotlib.pyplot as pl
X = np.linspace(-np.pi, np.pi, 256, endpoint=True)
```

```
CP = np.cos(X)
SP= np.sin(X)
pl.figure(figsize=(10,6), dpi=80)
pl.xlim(X.min()*1.5, X.max()*1.5)
pl.ylim(CP.min()*1.5, CP.max()*1.5)
pl.xticks([-np.pi, -np.pi/2, 0, np.pi/2, np.pi],
    [r'$-\pi$', r'$-\pi/2$', r'$0$', r'$+\pi/2$', r'$+\pi$'])

pl.yticks([-1, 0, +1],
    [r'$-1$', r'$0$', r'$+1$'])
axs = pl.gca()
axs.spines['right'].set_color('none')
axs.spines['top'].set_color('none')
axs.xaxis.set_ticks_position('bottom')
axs.spines['bottom'].set_position(('data',0))
axs.yaxis.set_ticks_position('left')
axs.spines['left'].set_position(('data',0))

pl.plot(X, CP, color="blue", linewidth=2.5, linestyle="-", label="cosine")
pl.plot(X, SP, color="red", linewidth=2.5, linestyle="-", label="sine")
pl.legend(loc='upper left', frameon=False)

pl.show()
```

3.3.4 Figures, Subplots, Axes and Ticks

In above example python have used implicit figure and axes creation. We can have more control over the display using figure, subplot, and axes explicitly. A figure in matplotlib means the whole window where plot is displayed in the user interface.

Within this figure there can be one or more subplots. Default is subplot (111).This means only one subplot in figure can be drawn. Subplot positions the plots in regular grid.

Axes allows the placement of subplots .The values (scale) displayed on axis is called ticks. When we call plot, matplotlib calls gca() to get the current axes and gca in turn calls gcf() to get the current figure.

Figure:

A figure is the interface in Matplotlib has "Figure #" as title. Figures are numbered starting from 1. There are several parameters whose default values are given below:-

Argument	Default	Description
Num	1	number of figure in interface
Figsize	figure.figsize	Width and height of figure size in inches
Dpi	figure.dpi	dots per inch (resolution of figure)
Facecolor	figure.facecolor	Background color of interface
edgecolor	figure.edgecolor	color of edge around the drawing background
Frameon	True	draw figure frame or not

The defaults are specified in the resource file and are used most of the time. Figures can be closed by clicking on the x in the upper right corner. But we can close a figure programmatically by calling close (). Depending on the argument it closes the current figure or a specific figure or all figures . Figure properties can be with the set_something methods.

Subplots

With subplot you can arrange plots in a regular grid. You need to specify the number of rows and columns and the number of the plot.
Example: Program that will draw two subplots in a figure and write heading in centre of plot.

```
from pylab import *
subplot(2,1,1)
xticks([]), yticks([])           #No x and y ticks
text(0.5,0.5, 'subplot(2,1,1)',ha='center',va='center',size=24,alpha=.5)

subplot(2,1,2)
xticks([]), yticks([])
text(0.5,0.5, 'subplot(2,1,2)',ha='center',va='center',size=24,alpha=.5)
show()
```

[Figure: subplot(2,1,1) above subplot(2,1,2)]

Axes

Axes are similar to subplots but allow placement of plots at any location in the figure. So if a smaller plot is to put inside a bigger one, we can do so this with axes.

```
from pylab import *
axes([0.1,0.1,.8,.8])
xticks([]), yticks([])
text(0.6,0.6,
'axes([0.1,0.1,.8,.8])',ha='center',va='center',size=20,alpha=.5)

axes([0.2,0.2,.3,.3])
xticks([]), yticks([])
text(0.5,0.5,
'axes([0.2,0.2,.3,.3])',ha='center',va='center',size=16,alpha=.5)
show()
```

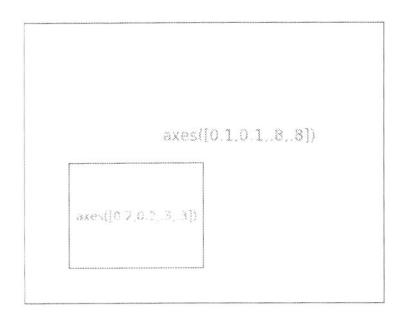

[Figure: axes([0.1,0.1,.8,.8]) containing axes([0.2,0.2,.3,.3])]

Ticks:

Ticks are label to show scale on axis. These make plots more clear to understand. Matplotlib provides a totally configurable system for ticks. Tick locators are used to specify where ticks should appear and tick formatters to customise ticks appearance. Major and minor ticks can be located and formatted independently from each other..

Tick Locators

There are several locators classes and description:

Class	Description
NullLocator	No ticks.
IndexLocator	Place a tick on every multiple of some base number of points plotted.
FixedLocator	Tick locations are fixed.
LinearLocator	Determine the tick locations.
MultipleLocator	Set a tick on every integer that is multiple of some base.
AutoLocator	Select no more than n intervals at nice locations.
LogLocator	Determine the tick locations for log axes.

[Python for Data Analysis]

CHAPTER 4: PANDAS

Pandas is a package in Python provides data structures which works with relational or labelled data in fast, flexible, and expressive way. It provides fundamental high-level building block real world data analysis . Additionally, it has powerful and flexible open source data analysis / manipulation tool .Pandas is well suited for Tabular data with heterogeneously-typed columns , ordered and unordered (not necessarily fixed-frequency) time series data, observational / statistical data sets.

4.1 Installing Pandas

Windows:
Pandas can be installed via pip from PyPI. Command pip is to executed on windows command prompt.
 pip install pandas
Linux:

To install pandas for Python 3 you may need to use the package python3-pandas.
sudo apt-get install python-pandas

4.2 Object Creation, Selection & Indexing

4.2.1 Object Creation Series & Data Frame

There are two primary data structures of pandas
1. Series (1-dimensional)
2. DataFrame (2-dimensional)

Example 1: Creating a Series by passing a list of values, letting pandas to create a default integer index:

```
import pandas as pd
import numpy as np
import matplotlib.pyplot as plt
s = pd.Series([1,np.nan,5,np.nan,6,8])
s
```
Output:
```
0    1.0
1    NaN
2    5.0
3    NaN
4    6.0
5    8.0
dtype: float64
```

Creating a DataFrame with a starting date and periods :
```
>>> dates = pd.date_range('20170101', periods=4)
>>> dates
DatetimeIndex(['2017-01-01', '2017-01-02', '2017-01-03', '2017-01-04'],
dtype='datetime64[ns]', freq='D')
```

Create dataframe by passing a numpy array, index and column label.
```
>>> df = pd.DataFrame(np.random.randn(4,4), index=dates,
columns=list('XYZW'))
>>> df
                X         Y         Z         W
2017-01-01  -1.587228 -0.385051 -0.264195  2.376143
2017-01-02   0.769625 -1.937781 -1.524778  0.936422
2017-01-03   0.550432  0.191810  0.569834 -1.618321
2017-01-04   1.142272 -1.207664 -1.486163 -0.417135
```

Creating a DataFrame which is collection of series by generating column wise values.

```
df2 = pd.DataFrame({ 'A' : 10.,
    ....:         'B' : pd.Timestamp('20170101'),
    ....:         'C' : pd.Series(1,index=list(range(4)),dtype='float32'),
    ....:         'D' : np.array([4] * 4,dtype='int32'),
    ....:         'E' : pd.Categorical(["A1","B1","A1","B1"]),
    ....:         'F' : 'test' })
df2
Output:
```

	A	B	C	D	E	F
0	10.0	2017-01-01	1.0	4	A1	test
1	10.0	2017-01-01	1.0	4	B1	test
2	10.0	2017-01-01	1.0	4	A1	test
3	10.0	2017-01-01	1.0	4	B1	test

Correlation

The Series object has a method cov to compute covariance between series (excluding NA/null values).
In [5]: s1 = pd.Series(np.random.randn(1000))
In [6]: s2 = pd.Series(np.random.randn(1000))
In [7]: s1.cov(s2)
Out[7]: 0.00068010881743110871
Analogously, DataFrame has a method cov to compute pairwise covariances among the series in the DataFrame, also excluding NA/null values.

4.2.2 Viewing Data/ Lookups Data Frames

```
df.head()
Output:
```

	X	Y	Z	W
2017-01-01	-1.587228	-0.385051	-0.264195	2.376143
2017-01-02	0.769625	-1.937781	-1.524778	0.936422
2017-01-03	0.550432	0.191810	0.569834	-1.618321
2017-01-04	1.142272	-1.207664	-1.486163	-0.417135

```
df.tail(2)    #display last two rows
Output:
```

	X	Y	Z	W
2017-01-03	0.550432	0.191810	0.569834	-1.618321

| 2017-01-04 | 1.142272 | -1.207664 | -1.486163 | -0.417135 |

4.2.3 Sorting by an Axis

```
>>> df.sort_index(axis=0)
```
	X	Y	Z	W
2017-01-01	-1.587228	-0.385051	-0.264195	2.376143
2017-01-02	0.769625	-1.937781	-1.524778	0.936422
2017-01-03	0.550432	0.191810	0.569834	-1.618321
2017-01-04	1.142272	-1.207664	-1.486163	-0.417135

```
>>> df.sort_index(axis=1)
```
	W	X	Y	Z
2017-01-01	2.376143	-1.587228	-0.385051	-0.264195
2017-01-02	0.936422	0.769625	-1.937781	-1.524778
2017-01-03	-1.618321	0.550432	0.191810	0.569834
2017-01-04	-0.417135	1.142272	-1.207664	-1.486163

4.2.4 Selection by Label

```
>>> df.loc[dates[0]]
X   -1.587228
Y   -0.385051
Z   -0.264195
W    2.376143
Name: 2017-01-01 00:00:00, dtype: float64
```

4.2.5 Selecting on a Multi-axis by Label

```
>>> df.loc[:,['X','Z']]
```
	X	Z
2017-01-01	-1.587228	-0.264195
2017-01-02	0.769625	-1.524778
2017-01-03	0.550432	0.569834
2017-01-04	1.142272	-1.486163

Showing label slicing, both endpoints are *included*
```
>>> df.loc['20170102':'20170104',['X','Z']]
```
	X	Z
2017-01-02	0.769625	-1.524778
2017-01-03	0.550432	0.569834
2017-01-04	1.142272	-1.486163

Reduction in the dimensions of the returned object

```
>>> df.loc['20170102',['X','Z']]
X   0.769625
Z  -1.524778
Name: 2017-01-02 00:00:00, dtype: float64
```

For getting a scalar value
To display 0th row X value
```
>>> df.loc[dates[0],'X']
-1.5872280521014948
```

4.2.6 Selection by Position

```
>>> df.iloc[3]
X   1.142272
Y  -1.207664
Z  -1.486163
W  -0.417135
Name: 2017-01-04 00:00:00, dtype: float64
```

For slicing rows explicitly
Display 1st to 4th row and all columns
```
>>> df.iloc[1:4,:]
```

	X	Y	Z	W
2017-01-02	0.769625	-1.937781	-1.524778	0.936422
2017-01-03	0.550432	0.191810	0.569834	-1.618321
2017-01-04	1.142272	-1.207664	-1.486163	-0.417135

For slicing columns explicitly
```
>>> df.iloc[:,1:2]
                Y
2017-01-01   -0.385051
2017-01-02   -1.937781
2017-01-03    0.191810
2017-01-04   -1.207664
```

For getting a particular [row,col] value
```
>>> df.iloc[1,1]
-1.9377809698716892
```

4.3 Handling NaN values

"Missing" means null or "data is not present". Many values in data sets are missing, either because it exists but not collected or it never existed. For example, in a data stream data is continuously generated and stored but to due to fault in data generation system for a duration, null valued will be stored in data.

In pandas, missing data can be introduced into a data set is by reindexing. For example

```
>>> df=pd.DataFrame(np.random.randn(3, 3), index=['a', 'c', 'e'],columns=['one', 'two', 'three'])
>>> df
        one         two         three
a    0.017773    2.439185    1.742292
c   -0.241506   -0.337997   -0.085486
e    0.243921   -1.319479    0.412318

>>> df2 = df.reindex(['a', 'b', 'c', 'd', 'e'])
>>> df2
        one         two         three
a    0.017773    2.439185    1.742292
b    NaN         NaN         NaN
c   -0.241506   -0.337997   -0.085486
d    NaN         NaN         NaN
e    0.243921   -1.319479    0.412318
```

Detecting Missing Data

To detecting missing values across different data types, pandas provides the isnull() and notnull() functions, which are applicable on Series and DataFrame objects:

```
>>> df2['one']
a    0.017773
b    NaN
c   -0.241506
d    NaN
e    0.243921
Name: one, dtype: float64

>>> pd.isnull(df2['one'])
a    False
b    True
c    False
d    True
e    False
```

Name: one, dtype: bool

```
>>> df2['one'].notnull()
a    True
b    False
c    True
d    False
e    True
Name: one, dtype: bool

>>> df2.isnull()
     one    two    three
a    False  False  False
b    True   True   True
c    False  False  False
d    True   True   True
e    False  False  False
```

4.4 Mapping

Map values of Series from source which can be a dictionary, Series, or function and returns series with same index as source.

    y=Series.map(arg, na_action=None)[source]

    arg : function, dictionary , or Series
    na_action : {None, 'ignore'}
If 'ignore', propagate NAN values, without passing them to the mapping function
y : Series
Examples
Map inputs series to output

```
>>> s = pd.Series([1,2,3], index=['one', 'two', 'three'])
>>> s
one      1
two      2
three    3
dtype: int64
>>> t = pd.Series(['map1', 'map2', 'map3'], index=[1,2,3])
>>> t
1    map1
2    map2
3    map3
```

```
dtype: object
>>> s.map(t)
one      map1
two      map2
three    map3
dtype: object
```

Use na_action to control when NAN values occur. None will not nothing and ignore will stop display of argument value.

```
>>> s = pd.Series([1, 2, 3, np.nan])
>>> t1 = s.map('this is a test string {}'.format, na_action=None)
0    this is a test string 1.0
1    this is a  test string 2.0
2    this is a  test string 3.0
3    this is a test  string nan
dtype: object
>>> t2 = s.map('this is a string {}'.format, na_action='ignore')
0    this is a test  string 1.0
1    this is a test string 2.0
2    this is a test  string 3.0
3              NaN
dtype: object
```

4.5 Reading Files

Create a File in Python in a Directory say C:\Users\HP\Desktop\python\

test.txt

I am a test file.
How long will you take to read me.

To read a file from a specific location, set path and read file
Example

```
Import os
>>> path = os.path.expanduser('~/Desktop/python/test.txt')
>>> path
'C:\\Users\\HP/Desktop/python/test.txt'

f = open(path, "r") #opens file with name of "test.txt"
```

The "r" tells Python that we want to read.

[Python for Data Analysis]   73

Python File Reading Methods

file.read(n) - This method reads n number of characters from the file, or if n is blank it reads the entire file.

file.readline(n) - This method reads a line from the text file till EOL.

    >>> print(f.read(1))
    I
    >>>print(f.read())
    am a test file.
    How long will you take to read me.

First, we open the file with f.open(). Then read(1) will read one character from file Python prints out "I". Next read() does not provide any arguments. But, it doesn't include that "I" that just read. Because read file is sequential process. Next read will start from current pointer.

Example

    f = open(path,"r") #opens file with name of "test.txt"
    print(f.readline())
    print(f.readline())

    Output:

    I am a test file.
    How long will you take to read me.

readline() method is used twice, we knew that we will get first 2 lines . Of course, we also knew that readline() reads only a line.

Example

    f = open(path,"r") #opens file with name of "test.txt"
    myLine = []
    for line in f:
       myLine.append(line)
    print(myLine)

    Output
    ['I am a test file.\n', '\n', 'How long will you take to read me.\n']

We open the file like normal, and we create a list.Then, we break the file into lines in our for loop using the in keyword. As we are looping through each line of the file we use myLine.append(line) to add each line to our myLine list.

Print() broke each line of the file into a string, which we can manipulate to do whatever we want
At end that you should always close your files
f.close()

4.6 Plot

Python can draw plots by using Matplotlib library. Data can be generated using series function of Pandas.

```
import pandas as pd
import numpy as np
import matplotlib.pyplot as plt
import matplotlib
matplotlib.style.use('ggplot')
t = pd.Series(np.random.randn(100), index=pd.date_range('1/1/2017', periods=100))  #generated data on 15 May 2017.
t = t.cumsum()
t.plot()
plt.show()
```

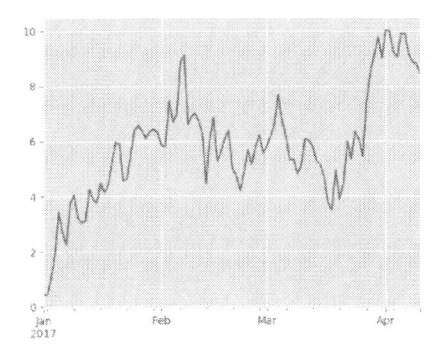

On DataFrame, to plot all of the columns with labels:

```
import pandas as pd
import numpy as np
import matplotlib.pyplot as plt
import matplotlib
matplotlib.style.use('ggplot')
t = pd.Series(np.random.randn(100), index=pd.date_range('1/1/2017', periods=100))
```

[Python for Data Analysis] 75

```
d = pd.DataFrame(np.random.randn(100, 4), index=t.index,
columns=list('XYZW'))
d = d.cumsum()
plt.figure(); d.plot(); plt.show()
```

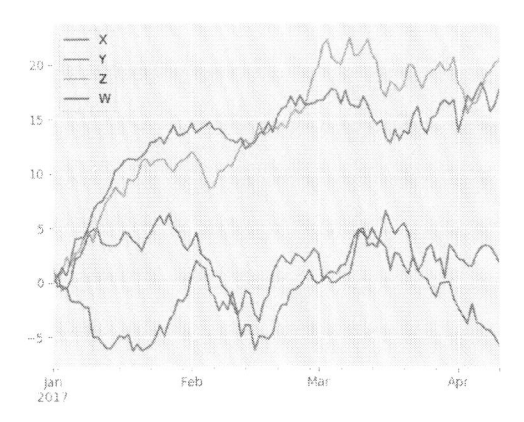

4.7 JOINS

Pandas can combine together Series, DataFrame, and Panel objects with various kinds of set logic and relational algebra functionality in the case of join / merge-type operations.

Concatenating objects

The concat function can perform concatenation operations along an axis while performing optional set logic (union or intersection) of the indexes (if any) on the other axes

```
import pandas as pd
import numpy as np
import matplotlib.pyplot as plt
import matplotlib
df1 = pd.DataFrame({'A': ['A0', 'A1', 'A2'],'B': ['B0', 'B1', 'B2'], 'C': ['C0',
'C1', 'C2'] }, index=[0, 1, 2])
df2 = pd.DataFrame({'A': ['A3', 'A4', 'A5'], 'B': ['B3', 'B4', 'B5'],'C': ['C3',
'C4', 'C5'], 'D': ['D3', 'D4', 'D5']},index=[3, 4, 5])
```

```
df3 = pd.DataFrame({'A': ['A6', 'A7', 'A8'], 'B': ['B6', 'B7', 'B8'], 'C': ['C6',
'C7', 'C8'], 'D': ['D6', 'D7', 'D8']}, index=[6, 7, 8])
frames = [df1, df2, df3]
result = pd.concat(frames)
print(result)
```

Output:
```
   A   B   C    D
0  A0  B0  C0  NaN
1  A1  B1  C1  NaN
2  A2  B2  C2  NaN
3  A3  B3  C3   D3
4  A4  B4  C4   D4
5  A5  B5  C5   D5
6  A6  B6  C6   D6
7  A7  B7  C7   D7
8  A8  B8  C8   D8
```

4.8 Histograms

Histogram can be drawn by using the function DataFrame and Series.plot.hist() methods.

```
import pandas as pd
import numpy as np
import matplotlib.pyplot as plt
import matplotlib
df4 = pd.DataFrame({'a': np.random.randn(100)+1, 'b':
np.random.randn(100), 'c': np.random.randn(100)-1, 'd':
np.random.randn(100)-2}, columns=['a', 'b', 'c', 'd'])
plt.figure();
df4.plot.hist(alpha=0.5)
plt.show()
```

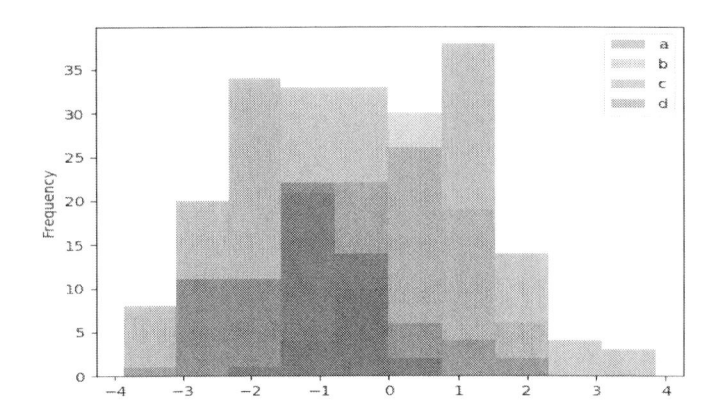

df4.plot.hist(stacked=True, bins=20)
df4.plot.hist(stacked=True, bins=20)

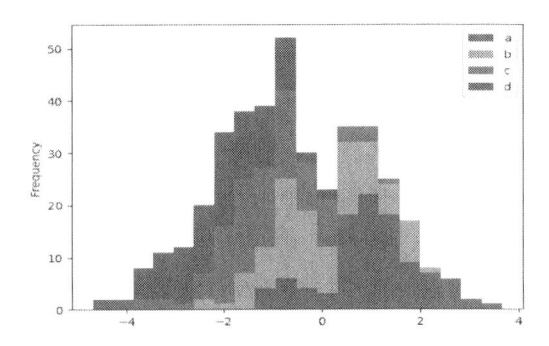

Rolling Calculations

```
>>> df = pd.DataFrame({'B': [0, 1, 2, np.nan, 4]})
>>> df
     B
0  0.0
1  1.0
2  2.0
3  NaN
4  4.0
```

Rolling sum with a window length of 2, using the 'triang' window type.

```
>>> df.rolling(2, win_type='triang').sum()
     B
```

```
0 NaN
1 1.0
2 2.5
3 NaN
4 NaN
```

Rolling sum with a window length of 2, min_periods defaults to the window length.

```
>>> df.rolling(2).sum()
     B
0 NaN
1 1.0
2 3.0
3 NaN
4 NaN
```

4.9 Date Time Index

pandas has proven to be successful as a tool for working with date and time series data, especially in the financial data analysis, big data or data mining.
In working with time series data, we can generate sequences of fixed-frequency dates and time spans, convert time series to a particular frequency or compute "relative" dates based on various non-standard time increments.

Create a range of dates:
# 24 hours starting with Jan 1st, 2017
rng = pd.date_range('1/1/2017', periods=72, freq='H')
rng[:5]
print(rng)
Output:
DatetimeIndex(['2017-01-01 00:00:00', '2017-01-01 01:00:00',
       '2017-01-01 02:00:00', '2017-01-01 03:00:00',
       '2017-01-01 04:00:00', '2017-01-01 05:00:00',
       '2017-01-01 06:00:00', '2017-01-01 07:00:00',
       '2017-01-01 08:00:00', '2017-01-01 09:00:00',
       '2017-01-01 10:00:00', '2017-01-01 11:00:00',
       '2017-01-01 12:00:00', '2017-01-01 13:00:00',
       '2017-01-01 14:00:00', '2017-01-01 15:00:00',
       '2017-01-01 16:00:00', '2017-01-01 17:00:00',
       '2017-01-01 18:00:00', '2017-01-01 19:00:00',
       '2017-01-01 20:00:00', '2017-01-01 21:00:00',

'2017-01-01 22:00:00', '2017-01-01 23:00:00'],
dtype='datetime64[ns]', freq='H')

Index pandas objects with dates:
Indexes can be generated along with dates by specifying index parameter in Pandas.series() function.

```
ts = pd.Series(np.random.randn(len(rng)), index=rng)
ts.head()
print(ts)
Output:
2017-01-01 00:00:00    -0.328165
2017-01-01 01:00:00    -0.043818
2017-01-01 02:00:00     0.874095
2017-01-01 03:00:00    -0.222245
.
.
.
Freq: H, dtype: float64
```

Change frequency and fill gaps:
```
# Change frequency to 45 minute and fill data
converted = ts.asfreq('45Min', method='pad')
converted.head()
print(converted)
Output:
2011-01-01 00:00:00     0.469112
2011-01-01 00:45:00     0.469112
2011-01-01 01:30:00    -0.282863
2011-01-01 02:15:00    -1.509059
2011-01-01 03:00:00    -1.135632
.
.

Freq: 45T, dtype: float64
```

Resample: Calculate Daily mean
```
ts.resample('D').mean()
Output
2017-01-01    0.286062
Freq: D, dtype: float6
```

4.10 Group By

- Aggregation: It computes aggregate summary statistics about each group. Like:-
    - Compute group average or sum
    - Compute group counts
- Transformation: perform some group-specific transformations and computer over a specific group. Example:-
    - Standardizing data (zscore) within group
    - Filling NAN within groups with a value
- Filtration: select some groups according to a group-wise computation.Example:-
    - Discarding some groups based on certain criteria
    - Filtering out groups based on the group aggregate sum or average.

You can display either aggregate information or columns on which groups are formed by using SELECT clause.

SELECT Column1, Column2, sum(Column3), count(Column4)
FROM Table1
GROUP BY Column1, Column2

Splitting an object into groups

pandas objects can be split on any of their axes. The abstract definition of grouping is to provide a mapping of labels to group names. To create a GroupBy object, you do the following:

```
>>> grouped = obj.groupby(key)
>>> grouped = obj.groupby(key, axis=1)
>>> grouped = obj.groupby([key1, key2])
```

Example, consider the following DataFrame for student data consist of

df = pd.DataFrame({'A' : ['std1', 'std2', 'std3', 'std1', 'std2', 'std1'], 'B' : ['A1', 'B1', 'C1', 'A2', 'B2', 'A3'], 'C' : [6,7,8,6,7,6]})
print(df)
Output

	A	B	C
0	std1	A1	6
1	std2	B1	7
2	std3	C1	8
3	std1	A2	6
4	std2	B2	7
5	std1	A3	6

To group above data on column A
```
grouped_df = df.groupby('A')
for key, item in grouped_df:
   print (grouped_df.get_group(key), "\n\n")
```

```
     A    B  C
0  std1  A1  6
3  std1  A2  6
5  std1  A3  6
     A    B  C
1  std2  B1  7
4  std2  B2  7


     A    B  C
2  std3  C1  8
```
To print groupwise sum
print (grouped_df.sum())
```
        C
A
std1   18
std2   14
std3    8
```

4.11 Aggregation

Once groups are created. We can perform aggregate function on groups.

```
print(grouped_df.aggregate(np.sum))
A
std1   18
std2   14
std3    8
```

Define multiple index for grouping:-
grouped_df = df.groupby(['A', 'B'])
grouped_df.aggregate(np.sum)
Output:

[Python for Data Analysis] 82

```
             C
  A    B
std1   A1    6
       A2    6
       A3    6
std2   B1    7
       B2    7
std3   C1    8
```

To describe statistics of a group:-
```
print(grouped_df.describe())
```
Output
```
                C
A
std1 count    3.0
     mean     6.0
     std      0.0
     min      6.0
     25%      6.0
     50%      6.0
     75%      6.0
     max      6.0
std2 count    2.0
     mean     7.0
     std      0.0
     min      7.0
     25%      7.0
     50%      7.0
     75%      7.0
     max      7.0
std3 count    1.0
     mean     8.0
     std      NaN
     min      8.0
     25%      8.0
     50%      8.0
     75%      8.0
     max      8.0
```

Pandas.io.data

Functions from pandas.io.data and pandas.io.ga extract data from various Internet sources into a DataFrame. Currently the following sources are supported:

[Python for Data Analysis]

Yahoo! Finance
Google Finance
St.Louis FED (FRED)
Kenneth French's data library
World Bank
Google Analytics

It should be noted, that various sources support different kinds of data, so not all sources implement the same methods and the data elements returned might also differ.

Yahoo! Finance

In [1]: import pandas.io.data as web
In [2]: import datetime
In [3]: start = datetime.datetime(2010, 1, 1)
In [4]: end = datetime.datetime(2013, 1, 27)
In [5]: f = web.DataReader("F", 'yahoo', start, end)
In [6]: f.ix['2010-01-04']
Out[6]:
Open   1.017000e+01
High   1.028000e+01
Low   1.005000e+01
Close   1.028000e+01
Volume   6.085580e+07
Adj Close 8.755953e+00
Name: 2010-01-04 00:00:00, dtype: float64

Panel

A panel is a 3D container of data. The term Panel data is derived from econometrics and is partially responsible for the name pandas − pan(el)-da(ta)-s.
The names for the 3 axes are intended to give some semantic meaning to describing operations involving panel data. They are −

items − axis 0, each item corresponds to a DataFrame contained inside.
major_axis − axis 1, it is the index (rows) of each of the DataFrames.
minor_axis − axis 2, it is the columns of each of the DataFrames.
pandas.Panel()
A Panel can be created using the following constructor −
pandas.Panel(data, items, major_axis, minor_axis, dtype, copy)
The parameters of the constructor are as follows −

Parameter   Description data   Data takes various forms like ndarray, series, map, lists, dict, constants and also another DataFrame
items   axis=0

major_axis	axis=1
minor_axis	axis=2
dtype	Data type of each column
copy	Copy data. Default, false

Create Panel

A Panel can be created using multiple ways like –
  From ndarrays
  From dict of DataFrames
  From 3D ndarray
  # creating an empty panel
  import pandas as pd
  import numpy as np
  data = np.random.rand(2,4,5)
  p = pd.Panel(data)
  print p
  Its output is as follows –

  <class 'pandas.core.panel.Panel'>
  Dimensions: 2 (items) x 4 (major_axis) x 5 (minor_axis)
  Items axis: 0 to 1
  Major_axis axis: 0 to 3
  Minor_axis axis: 0 to 4

Chapter 5: Suggested Practices

5.1 Suggested Programs

Program 1: Write Program in Python which count frequency of words in a given sentence.

#String as input to program

wordstring = 'it was the best of times it was the worst of times '
wordstring += 'it was the age of wisdom it was the age of foolishness'

#Extract words from string
wordlist = wordstring.split()

```
wordfreq = []

# Calculate word frequencies
for w in wordlist:
    wordfreq.append(wordlist.count(w))
print("String\n" + wordstring +"\n")
print("List\n" + str(wordlist) + "\n")
print("Frequencies\n" + str(wordfreq) + "\n")
print("Pairs\n" + str(zip(wordlist, wordfreq)))
```

Output :

String
it was the best of times it was the worst of times it was the age of wisdom it was the age of foolishness

List
['it', 'was', 'the', 'best', 'of', 'times', 'it', 'was', 'the', 'worst', 'of', 'times', 'it', 'was', 'the', 'age', 'of', 'wisdom', 'it', 'was', 'the', 'age', 'of', 'foolishness']

Frequencies
[4, 4, 4, 1, 4, 2, 4, 4, 4, 1, 4, 2, 4, 4, 4, 2, 4, 1, 4, 4, 4, 2, 4, 1]

Pairs
<zip object at 0x034AA0A8>

Program 2: Build the Hangman Game using Python.

This is a Python script of the classic game "Hangman". The word to guess is represented by a row of dashes. If the player guess a letter which exists in the word, the script writes it in all its correct positions. The player has 10 turns to guess the word. You can easily customize the game by changing the variables.

```
#importing the time module
import time

#welcoming the user
name = input('What is your name? ')

print ("Hello, " + name, "Time to play hangman!")
```

```python
print ("")

#wait for 1 second
time.sleep(1)

print ("Start guessing...")
time.sleep(0.5)


#here we set the secret
word = "secret"

#creates an variable with an empty value
guesses = ''

#determine the number of turns
turns = 10

# Create a while loop

#check if the turns are more than zero
while turns > 0:

    # make a counter that starts with zero
    failed = 0
    # for every character in secret_word
    for char in word:

    # see if the character is in the players guess
        if char in guesses:

        # print then out the character
            print (char)

        else:

        # if not found, print a dash
            print ("_")

        # and increase the failed counter with one
            failed += 1
```

```python
# if failed is equal to zero

# print You Won
if failed == 0:
    print ("You won")

    # exit the script
    break

# ask the user go guess a character
guess = input("guess a character:")

# set the players guess to guesses
guesses += guess
# if the guess is not found in the secret word
if guess not in word:

    # turns counter decreases with 1 (now 9)
    turns -= 1

    # print wrong
    print ("Wrong")

    # how many turns are left
    print ("You have", + turns, 'more guesses' )

    # if the turns are equal to zero
    if turns == 0:

        # print "You Loose"
        print ("You Loose")
```

Output:
What is your name? Peter
Hello, Peter Time to play hangman!

Start guessing...

_
_
_
_

[Python for Data Analysis]

_

_

guess a character:a
Wrong
You have 9 more guesses

_

_

_

_

_

guess a character:

Program 3: Write python code loads the any dataset (example.txt consist of comma separated data as given below), and plot the graph.

example.txt file data
1,5
2,3
3,4
4,7
5,4
6,3
7,5
8,7
9,4
10,4

.Txt file is stored in absolute location ~/Desktop/python/example.txt'. This program will read data from file and create plot on data.

#import libraries
import matplotlib.pyplot as plt
import os
import numpy as np

#Open file and load data in variable x.y
x = []
y = []
path = os.path.expanduser('~/Desktop/python/example.txt')
x, y = np.loadtxt(path, delimiter=',', unpack=True)

```
#Plot x,y
plt.plot(x,y, label='Loaded from file!')
plt.xlabel('x')
plt.ylabel('y')
plt.title('Interesting Graph\nCheck it out')
plt.legend()
plt.show()
```

Output:

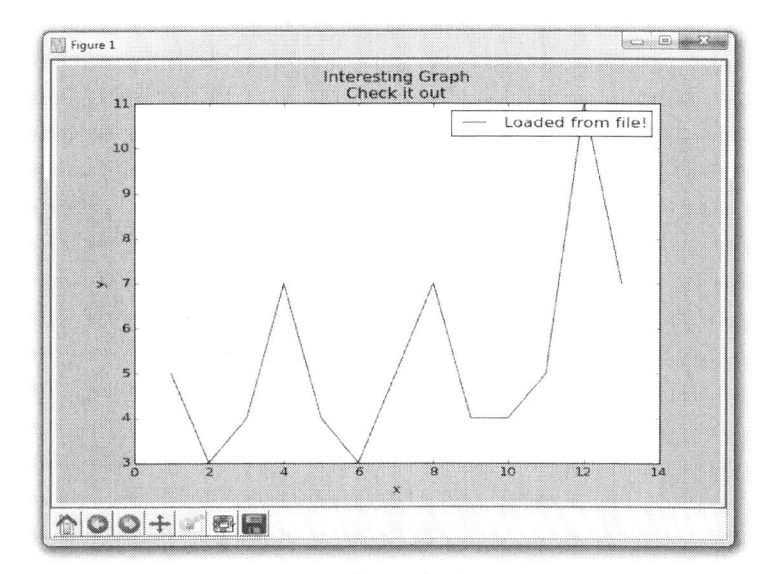

Program 4: Write python code loads the any dataset (example1.csv), and does some basic data cleaning. Add component on data set.

This program creates .csv file using data frames. It retrieves data from .csv file, add a row to data and write updated contents back to .csv file. Updating also required to be through data frames.

```
import pandas as pd
import numpy as np
import os

#Create data frame
raw_data = {'first_name': ['Jason', 'Molly', 'Tina', 'Jake', 'Amy'],
    'last_name': ['Miller', 'Jacobson', ".", 'Milner', 'Cooze'],
    'age': [42, 52, 36, 24, 73],
```

```
'preTestScore': [4, 24, 31, ".", "."],
'postTestScore': ["25,000", "94,000", 57, 62, 70]}
df = pd.DataFrame(raw_data, columns = ['first_name', 'last_name', 'age',
'preTestScore', 'postTestScore'])

# Create file '~/Desktop/python/example1.csv and Write Dataframe
path = os.path.expanduser('~/Desktop/python/')
df.to_csv(path + 'example1.csv')
df = pd.read_csv(path + 'example1.csv')

#Add new row at end and write dataframe back to file
idx = len(df)
df.loc[idx] = [5,'Ram','Peter',34,5,80]
df.to_csv(path + 'example1.csv')
Output:
Contents of example1.csv
```

	Unnamed: 0	first_name	last_name	age	preTestScore	postTestScore
0	0	Jason	Miller	42	4	25,000
1	1	Molly	Jacobson	52	24	94,000
2	2	Tina	.	36	31	57
3	3	Jake	Milner	24	.	62
4	4	Amy	Cooze	73	.	70
5	5	Ram	Peter	34	5	80

5.2 Mini Project

1. Implementing a simple Recommender System based on user buying pattern.
2. Twitter Sentiment Analysis in Python
3. Applying linear regression model to a real world problem.

1. Implementing a simple Recommender System based on buying patters.

Recommendation engines are nothing but an automated form of a "shop counter guy". You ask system for a product, It not only shows that product, but also the related ones which one could buy. They are well trained in cross selling and up selling.

The ability of these engines to recommend personalized content, based on past behavior is incredible. It brings customer delight and gives them a reason to keep returning to the website.

Recommend the most popular items

A simple approach could be to recommend the items which are liked by most number of users. Basically the most popular items would be same for each user since popularity is defined on the entire user pool. So everybody will see the same results. It sounds like, 'a website recommends you to buy microwave just because it's been liked by other users .

Surprisingly, such approach still works in places like news portals. Whenever you login to say bbcnews, you'll see a column of "Popular News" which is subdivided into sections and the most read articles of each sections are displayed.

We will be using the MovieLens dataset for this purpose. It has been collected by the GroupLens Research Project at the University of Minnesota. MovieLens 100K dataset can be downloaded from
https://grouplens.org/datasets/movielens/100k/. It consists of:

- **100,000 ratings** (1-5) from 943 users on 1682 movies.
- Each user has rated **at least 20 movies.**
- Simple demographic info for the users (age, gender, occupation, zip)
- Genre information of movies
- It consist of following files
- u.data   -- The full u data set, 100000 ratings by 943 users on 1682 items.Each user has rated at least 20 movies. Users and items are numbered consecutively from 1. The data is randomly ordered. This is a tab separated list of user id | item id | rating | timestamp. The time stamps are unix seconds since 1/1/1970 UTC
- u.info   -- The number of users, items, and ratings in the u data set.
- u.item   -- Information about the items (movies); this is a tab separated list of movie id | movie title | release date | video release date |IMDb URL | unknown | Action | Adventure | Animation | Children's | Comedy | Crime | Documentary | Drama | Fantasy |Film-Noir | Horror | Musical | Mystery | Romance | Sci-Fi |Thriller | War | Western |
- The last 19 fields are the genres, a 1 indicates the movie is of that genre, a 0 indicates it is not; movies can be in
- several genres at once.The movie ids are the ones used in the u.data data set.
- u.user   -- Demographic information about the users; this is a tab
- separated list of user id | age | gender | occupation | zip code

[Python for Data Analysis]   92

- The user ids are the ones used in the u.data data set.
- ua.base -- The data sets ua.base, ua.test, ub.base, and ub.test
- ua.test split the u data into a training set and a test set with

Lets load this data into Python. There are many files in the **ml-100k.zip** file which we can use. Lets load the three most importance files to get a sense of the data.

```
import pandas as pd
import numpy as np
import os
import graphlab
from graphlab import SFrame

# pass in column names for each CSV and read them using pandas.
# Column names available in the readme file

#Reading users file:
u_cols = ['user_id', 'age', 'sex', 'occupation', 'zip_code']
path = os.path.expanduser('~/Desktop/python/ml-100k/u.user')
users = pd.read_csv(path, sep='|', names=u_cols,encoding='latin-1')

#Reading ratings file:
r_cols = ['user_id', 'movie_id', 'rating', 'unix_timestamp']
path = os.path.expanduser('~/Desktop/python/ml-100k/u.data')
ratings = pd.read_csv(path, sep='\t', names=r_cols,
 encoding='latin-1')

#Reading items file:
i_cols = ['movie id', 'movie title' ,'release date','video release date', 'IMDb URL', 'unknown', 'Action', 'Adventure',
 'Animation', 'Children\'s', 'Comedy', 'Crime', 'Documentary', 'Drama', 'Fantasy',
 'Film-Noir', 'Horror', 'Musical', 'Mystery', 'Romance', 'Sci-Fi', 'Thriller', 'War', 'Western']
path = os.path.expanduser('~/Desktop/python/ml-100k/u.item')
items = pd.read_csv(path, sep='|', names=i_cols,
 encoding='latin-1')
```

This reconfirms that there are 943 users and we have 5 features for each namely their unique ID, age, gender, occupation and the zip code they are living in.

```
print (users.shape)
users.head()
```

[Python for Data Analysis]

This confirms that there are 100K ratings for different user and movie combinations. Also notice that each rating has a timestamp associated with it.

    print (ratings.shape)
    ratings.head()

This dataset contains attributes of the 1682 movies. There are 24 columns out of which 19 specify the genre of a particular movie. The last 19 columns are for each genre and a value of 1 denotes movie belongs to that genre and 0 otherwise.

    print (items.shape)
    items.head()

Now we have to divide the ratings data set into test and train data for making models. Luckily GroupLens provides pre-divided data wherein the test data has 10 ratings for each user, i.e. 9430 rows in total. Lets load that:

    r_cols = ['user_id', 'movie_id', 'rating', 'unix_timestamp']
    path = os.path.expanduser('~/Desktop/python/ml-100k/ua.base')
    ratings_base = pd.read_csv(path, sep='\t', names=r_cols, encoding='latin-1')
    path = os.path.expanduser('~/Desktop/python/ml-100k/ua.test')
    ratings_test = pd.read_csv(path, sep='\t', names=r_cols, encoding='latin-1')
    print(ratings_base.shape)
    print(ratings_test.shape)

Since we'll be using GraphLab, lets convert these in SFrames..

    train_data = graphlab.SFrame(ratings_base)
    test_data = graphlab.SFrame(ratings_test)

Lets start with making a popularity based model, i.e. the one where all the users have same recommendation based on the most popular choices. We'll use the graphlab recommender functions popularity_recommender for this. We can train a recommendation as:

    popularity_model = graphlab.popularity_recommender.create(train_data, user_id='user_id', item_id='movie_id', target='rating')
    #Get recommendations for first 5 users and print them
    #users = range(1,6) specifies user ID of first 5 users
    #k=5 specifies top 5 recommendations to be given
    popularity_recomm = popularity_model.recommend(users=range(1,6),k=5)
    popularity_recomm.print_rows(num_rows=25)
    Output:
    943, 5)
    (100000, 4)
    (100000, 4)
    (1682, 24)
    (90570, 4)

[Python for Data Analysis] 94

(9430, 4)
Recsys training: model = popularity
Warning: Ignoring columns unix_timestamp;
To use these columns in scoring predictions, use a model that allows the use of additional features.
Preparing data set.
    Data has 90570 observations with 943 users and 1680 items.
    Data prepared in: 0.152106s
90570 observations to process; with 1680 unique items.

user_id	movie_id	score	rank
1	1467	5.0	1
1	1201	5.0	2
1	1189	5.0	3
1	1122	5.0	4
1	814	5.0	5
2	1467	5.0	1
2	1201	5.0	2
2	1189	5.0	3
2	1122	5.0	4
2	814	5.0	5
3	1467	5.0	1
3	1201	5.0	2
3	1189	5.0	3
3	1122	5.0	4
3	814	5.0	5
4	1467	5.0	1
4	1201	5.0	2
4	1189	5.0	3
4	1122	5.0	4
4	814	5.0	5
5	1467	5.0	1
5	1201	5.0	2
5	1189	5.0	3
5	1122	5.0	4
5	814	5.0	5

[25 rows x 4 columns]

To execute this practical graphlab can be downloaded from
ttps://turi.com/download/install-graphlab-create-command-line.html

Step 1: Download Anaconda2 v4.0.0

Step 2: Install Anaconda
Run Anaconda2 v4.0.0 installer.
Double-click the .exe file to install Anaconda and follow the instructions on the screen.

Step 3: Create conda environment
Create a new conda environment with Python 2.7.x
conda create -n gl-env python=2.7 anaconda=4.0.0
Activate the conda environment
activate gl-env

Step 4: Ensure pip version >= 7
Ensure pip is updated to the latest version
miniconda users may need to install pip first, using 'conda install pip'
conda update pip

Step 5: Install GraphLab Create
Install your licensed copy of GraphLab Create
pip install --upgrade --no-cache-dir https://get.graphlab.com/GraphLab-Create/2.1/your registered email address here/your product key here/GraphLab-Create-License.tar.gz
Step 6: Ensure installation of IPython and IPython Notebook
Install or update IPython and IPython Notebook
conda install ipython-notebook

2.Twitter sentiment analysis in python.

What is sentiment analysis?
Sentiment Analysis is the process of 'computationally' determining whether a piece of writing is positive, negative or neutral. It's also known as **opinion mining**, deriving the opinion or attitude of a speaker.
Why sentiment analysis?
- **Business:** In marketing field companies use it to develop their strategies, to understand customers' feelings towards products or brand, how people respond to their campaigns or product launches and why consumers don't buy some products.

- **Politics:** In political field, it is used to keep track of political view, to detect consistency and inconsistency between statements and actions at the government level. It can be used to predict election results as well!
- **Public Actions:** Sentiment analysis also is used to monitor and analyse social phenomena, for the spotting of potentially dangerous situations and determining the general mood of the blogosphere.
- **Installation:**
- **Tweepy:** tweepy is the python client for the official Twitter API. Install it using following pip command:Pip install command is found in scripts directory of python directory. This command can be executed on command prompt.
  pip install tweepy
- **TextBlob:** textblob is the python library for processing textual data. Install it using following pip command:
  pip install textblob

Authentication:
In order to fetch tweets through Twitter API, one needs to register an App through their twitter account. Follow these steps for the same:
- Open this https://apps.twitter.com/ and click the button: 'Create New App'
- Fill the application details. You can leave the callback url field empty.
- Once the app is created, you will be redirected to the app page.
- Open the 'Keys and Access Tokens' tab.
- Copy 'Consumer Key', 'Consumer Secret', 'Access token' and 'Access Token Secret'.

Program:
```
import re
import tweepy
from tweepy import OAuthHandler
from textblob import TextBlob

class TwitterClient(object):
''' Generic Twitter Class for sentiment analysis.'''
def __init__(self):
'''Class constructor or initialization method.'''
consumer_key = 'XXXXXXXXXXXXXXXXXXXXXXXX'
consumer_secret = 'XXXXXXXXXXXXXXXXXXXXXXXXXXXX'
access_token = 'XXXXXXXXXXXXXXXXXXXXXXXXXX'
access_token_secret = 'XXXXXXXXXXXXXXXXXXXXXXXX'
# attempt authentication
```

```python
try:
    # create OAuthHandler object
    self.auth = OAuthHandler(consumer_key, consumer_secret)
    # set access token and secret
    self.auth.set_access_token(access_token, access_token_secret)
    # create tweepy API object to fetch tweets
    self.api = tweepy.API(self.auth)
except:
    print("Error: Authentication Failed")
def clean_tweet(self, tweet):
    '''Utility function to clean tweet text by removing links, special characters
    using simple regex statements.'''
    return ' '.join(re.sub("(@[A-Za-z0-9]+)|([^0-9A-Za-z \t])|(\w+:\/\/\S+)", " ",
        tweet).split())

def get_tweet_sentiment(self, tweet):
    '''Utility function to classify sentiment of passed tweet using textblob's sentiment method'''
    # create TextBlob object of passed tweet text
    analysis = TextBlob(self.clean_tweet(tweet))
    # set sentiment
    if analysis.sentiment.polarity > 0:
        return 'positive'
    elif analysis.sentiment.polarity == 0:
        return 'neutral'
    else:
        return 'negative'

def get_tweets(self, query, count = 10):
    ''' Main function to fetch tweets and parse them.'''
    # empty list to store parsed tweets
    tweets = []
    try:
        # call twitter api to fetch tweets
        fetched_tweets = self.api.search(q = query, count = count)
        # parsing tweets one by one
        for tweet in fetched_tweets:
            # empty dictionary to store required params of a tweet
            parsed_tweet = {}
            # saving text of tweet
            parsed_tweet['text'] = tweet.text
            # saving sentiment of tweet
```

```
parsed_tweet['sentiment'] = self.get_tweet_sentiment(tweet.text)
# appending parsed tweet to tweets list
if tweet.retweet_count > 0:
# if tweet has retweets, ensure that it is appended only once
if parsed_tweet not in tweets:
tweets.append(parsed_tweet)
else:
tweets.append(parsed_tweet)
# return parsed tweets
return tweets
except tweepy.TweepError as e:
# print error (if any)
print("Error : " + str(e))

def main():
        # creating object of TwitterClient Class
        api = TwitterClient()
        # calling function to get tweets
        tweets = api.get_tweets(query = 'modi', count = 20)
        # print(tweets)
        # picking positive tweets from tweets
        ptweets = [tweet for tweet in tweets if tweet['sentiment'] == 'positive' ]
        # percentage of positive tweets
        print("Positive tweets percentage: {} 
%".format(100*len(ptweets)/len(tweets)))
        # picking negative tweets from tweets
        ntweets = [tweet for tweet in tweets if tweet['sentiment'] == 'negative']
        # percentage of negative tweets
        print("Negative tweets percentage: {} 
%".format(100*len(ntweets)/len(tweets)))
        # percentage of neutral tweets
        #print("Neutral tweets percentage: {} %".format(100*len(tweets - 
ntweets - ptweets)/len(tweets)))
        # printing first 5 positive tweets
        print("\n\nPositive tweets:")
        for tweet in ptweets[:10]:
                print(tweet['text'])

        # printing first 5 negative tweets
        print("\n\nNegative tweets:")
        for tweet in ntweets[:10]:
                print(tweet['text'])
```

```
if __name__ == "__main__":
    # calling main function
    main()
```

Output
Positive tweets percentage: 36 %
Negative tweets percentage: 21 %
Positive tweets:
RT @YiTweets: Many #YoungIndians #Yi Members meet PM Modi in #ChampionsOfChange conference to drive & deliver change across 6 pillars of gr...
RT @GauravPandhi: ..in Japan, PM Modi literally laughed at the misery of Indians. "Ghar mein shaadi hai, paise nahi hain hahahaha" #Speechl...
RT @BoscoUnchained: #Demonetisation helped the rich and ruined the poor, even killed many of them.
In short, Modi's masterstroke worsened o...
RT @amitvarma: 2/x Here's my first piece after DeMon, comparing Modi to Tughlaq, & invoking Hayek to explain why it was a blunder: https://...
I liked a @YouTube video https://t.co/NC9BYCUK6H Lokpal को लेकर Modi के खिलाफ आंदोलन की
RT @ashu3page: Anna Hazare writes to PM Modi on the issue of Lokpal, says difference between your words & action. Anna warns agitation in D...
RT @56perumal: Demonetisation is a huge success, says the RBI Annual Report; This is how PM Modi will hunt down https://t.co/SvlxGIfqyx via...

Negative tweets:
#Modi a Corrupt☐?
99% Demonetised Notes Back in Sys:RBI
=Mlns Livelihoods Gone-2Save Cronies from Repaying Loans...
https://t.co/qM4U7BcMtP

RT @pawanjhawat: #JaagoRe देशवाशयो-

Modi gave us pink, blue & yellow money.
But Modi ji where is the #BlackMoney ?

@AshokTanwar_INC @Hasi...
99% of demonetized notes deposited to banks so where is the Black Money ?
Modi , u made 1.2 billion people hell in those couple of months.

[Python for Data Analysis]

RT @INCIndia: Despite tall claims by PM Modi, #demonetisation hardly made a dent in India's vast shadow economy.

3. Applying linear regression model to a real world problem.

Linear regression assumes a linear or straight line relationship between the input variables (X) and the single output variable (y).More specifically, that output (y) can be calculated from a linear combination of the input variables (X). When there is a single input variable, the method is referred to as a simple linear regression.In simple linear regression we can use statistics on the training data to estimate the coefficients required by the model to make predictions on new data.The line for a simple linear regression model can be written as:

Y=b0+b1*x

where b0 and b1 are the coefficients we must estimate from the training data. Once the coefficients are known, we can use this equation to estimate output values for y given new input examples of x.It requires that you calculate statistical properties from the data such as mean, variance and covariance. All the algebra has been taken care of and we are left with some arithmetic to implement to estimate the simple linear regression coefficients.

B1 = sum((x(i) - mean(x)) * (y(i) - mean(y))) / sum((x(i) - mean(x))^2)
B0 = mean(y) - B1 * mean(x)
where the i refers to the value of the i th value of the input x or output y.

Swedish Insurance Dataset

We will use a real dataset.The dataset is called the "Auto Insurance in Sweden" dataset and involves predicting the total payment for all the claims in thousands of Swedish Kronor (y) given the total number of claims (x).
This means that for a new number of claims (x) we will be able to predict the total payment of claims (y).
Example 5 record dataset
108,392.5
19,46.2
13,15.7
124,422.2
40,119.4

It can be downloaded from
http://college.cengage.com/mathematics/brase/understandable_statistics/7e/student
s/datasets/slr/frames/slr06.html

Make Predictions

The simple linear regression model is a line defined by coefficients estimated from training data. Once the coefficients are estimated, we can use them to make predictions. The equation to make predictions with a simple linear regression model is as follows:

$y = b0 + b1 * x$

function named simple_linear_regression() that implements the prediction equation to make predictions on a test dataset. It also ties together the estimation of the coefficients on training data from the steps above. The coefficients prepared from the training data are used to make predictions on the test data, which are then returned.

We will also add in a function to manage the evaluation of the predictions called evaluate_algorithm() and another function to estimate the Root Mean Squared Error of the predictions called rmse_metric().

Specifically a function to load the CSV file called load_csv(), a function to convert a loaded dataset to numbers called str_column_to_float(), a function to evaluate an algorithm using a train and test set called train_test_split() a function to calculate RMSE called rmse_metric() and a function to evaluate an algorithm called evaluate_algorithm().

The complete example is listed below.

A training dataset of 60% of the data is used to prepare the model and predictions are made on the remaining 40%.

```
# Simple Linear Regression on the Swedish Insurance Dataset
from random import seed
from random import randrange
from csv import reader
from math import sqrt
import matplotlib.pyplot as plt

# Load a CSV file
def load_csv(filename):
    dataset = list()
    with open(filename, 'r') as file:
        csv_reader = reader(file)
        for row in csv_reader:
```

```python
                if not row:
                    continue
                dataset.append(row)
    return dataset

# Convert string column to float
def str_column_to_float(dataset, column):
    for row in dataset:
        row[column] = float(row[column].strip())

# Split a dataset into a train and test set
def train_test_split(dataset, split):
    train = list()
    train_size = split * len(dataset)
    dataset_copy = list(dataset)
    while len(train) < train_size:
        index = randrange(len(dataset_copy))
        train.append(dataset_copy.pop(index))
    return train, dataset_copy

# Calculate root mean squared error
def rmse_metric(actual, predicted):
    sum_error = 0.0
    for i in range(len(actual)):
        prediction_error = predicted[i] - actual[i]
        sum_error += (prediction_error ** 2)
    mean_error = sum_error / float(len(actual))
    return sqrt(mean_error)

# Evaluate an algorithm using a train/test split
def evaluate_algorithm(dataset, algorithm, split, *args):
    train, test = train_test_split(dataset, split)
    test_set = list()
    for row in test:
        row_copy = list(row)
        row_copy[-1] = None
        test_set.append(row_copy)
    predicted = algorithm(train, test_set, *args)
    actual = [row[-1] for row in test]
    rmse = rmse_metric(actual, predicted)
    return rmse
```

```python
# Calculate the mean value of a list of numbers
def mean(values):
    return sum(values) / float(len(values))

# Calculate covariance between x and y
def covariance(x, mean_x, y, mean_y):
    covar = 0.0
    for i in range(len(x)):
        covar += (x[i] - mean_x) * (y[i] - mean_y)
    return covar

# Calculate the variance of a list of numbers
def variance(values, mean):
    return sum([(x-mean)**2 for x in values])

# Calculate coefficients
def coefficients(dataset):
    x = [row[0] for row in dataset]
    y = [row[1] for row in dataset]
    x_mean, y_mean = mean(x), mean(y)
    b1 = covariance(x, x_mean, y, y_mean) / variance(x, x_mean)
    b0 = y_mean - b1 * x_mean
    return [b0, b1]

# Simple linear regression algorithm
def simple_linear_regression(train, test):
    predictions = list()
    b0, b1 = coefficients(train)
    for row in test:
        yhat = b0 + b1 * row[0]
        predictions.append(yhat)
    return predictions

# Simple linear regression on insurance dataset
seed(1)
# load and prepare data
dataset = load_csv('insurance1.csv')
for i in range(len(dataset[0])):
    str_column_to_float(dataset, i)
# evaluate algorithm
split = 0.6
rmse = evaluate_algorithm(dataset, simple_linear_regression, split)
```

```
print('RMSE: %.3f' % (rmse))
x = [row[0] for row in dataset]
y = [row[1] for row in dataset]
print(x)
print(y)
plt.plot(x,y, label='Loaded from file!')
plt.show()
```

RMSE: 38.339
[108.0, 19.0, 13.0, 124.0, 40.0, 57.0, 23.0, 14.0, 45.0, 10.0, 5.0, 48.0, 11.0, 23.0, 7.0, 2.0, 24.0, 6.0, 3.0, 23.0, 6.0, 9.0, 9.0, 3.0, 29.0, 7.0, 4.0, 20.0, 7.0, 4.0, 0.0, 25.0, 6.0, 5.0, 22.0, 11.0, 61.0, 12.0, 4.0, 16.0, 13.0, 60.0, 41.0, 37.0, 55.0, 41.0, 11.0, 27.0, 8.0, 3.0, 17.0, 13.0, 13.0, 15.0, 8.0, 29.0, 30.0, 24.0, 9.0, 31.0, 14.0, 53.0, 26.0]
[392.5, 46.2, 15.7, 422.2, 119.4, 170.9, 56.9, 77.5, 214.0, 65.3, 20.9, 248.1, 23.5, 39.6, 48.8, 6.6, 134.9, 50.9, 4.4, 113.0, 14.8, 48.7, 52.1, 13.2, 103.9, 77.5, 11.8, 98.1, 27.9, 38.1, 0.0, 69.2, 14.6, 40.3, 161.5, 57.2, 217.6, 58.1, 12.6, 59.6, 89.9, 202.4, 181.3, 152.8, 162.8, 73.4, 21.3, 92.6, 76.1, 39.9, 142.1, 93.0, 31.9, 32.1, 55.6, 133.3, 194.5, 137.9, 87.4, 209.8, 95.5, 244.6, 187.5]

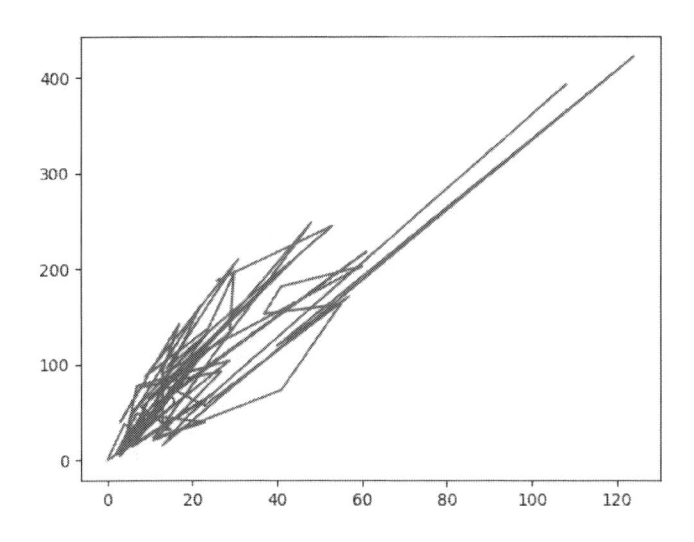

4. Language Data processing using the Natural Language Toolkit (NLTK)

Text-based communication has become one of the most common forms of expression. We email, text message, tweet, and update our statuses on a daily basis. As a result, unstructured text data has become extremely common, and analysing large quantities of text data is now a key way to understand what people are thinking. Python has Natural Language Tool kit (NLTK) , which helps to analyse text, providing a way for computers to understand human language. NLP applications such as automatic summarization, topic segmentation, and sentiment analysis etc can be developed using NLTK. Tweets on Twitter help us find trending news topics in the world. Reviews on Amazon help users purchase the best-rated products.

Prerequisites

For NLTKl, you should have Python 3 installed, as well as a local programming environment set up on your computer.

Step 1 — Importing NLTK

Before we begin working in Python, make sure that the NLTK module is installed. On the command line, check for NLTK by running the following command:
python -c "import nltk"
If NLTK is installed, this command will complete with no error. If NLTK is not installed, you will receive an error message. Make sure to install latest version:
python -c "import nltk; print(nltk.__version__)"
If NLTK is not installed, so download the library using pip:
pip install nltk

Step 2 — Downloading NLTK's Data and Tagger

Twitter corpus data can be downloaded through NLTK using command:
python -m nltk.downloader twitter_samples
Next, download the part-of-speech (POS) tagger. *POS tagging* is the process of labelling a word in a text as corresponding to a particular POS tag: nouns, verbs, adjectives, adverbs, etc.
python -m nltk.downloader averaged_perceptron_tagger
We can double check that the corpus downloaded correctly. In terminal, open up the Python interactive environment:

python

In Python's interactive environment, import the twitter_samples corpus:
from nltk.corpus import twitter_samples

[Python for Data Analysis] 106

NLTK's twitter corpus currently contains a sample of 20,000 tweets retrieved from the Twitter Streaming API. Full tweets are stored as line-separated JSON. We can see how many JSON files exist in the corpus using the twitter_samples.fileids() method:

twitter_samples.fileids()

Output will look like this:

Output

[u'negative_tweets.json', u'positive_tweets.json', u'tweets.20150430-223406.json']

Using those file IDs we can then return the tweet strings:

twitter_samples.strings('tweets.20150430-223406.json')

Running this will return a lot of output. It will generally look like this:

Output

[u'RT @KirkKus: Indirect cost of the UK being in the EU is estimated to be costing Britain \xa3170 billion per year! #BetterOffOut #UKIP'...]

Exit the Python interactive environment with the shortcut ctrl + D.and write the script to process tweets.

The goal of our script will be to count how many adjectives and nouns appear in the positive subset of the twitter_samples corpus:

- A noun, in its most basic definition, is usually defined as a person, place, or thing. For example, a *movie*, a *book*, and a *burger* are all nouns. Counting nouns can help determine how many different topics are being discussed.

- An adjective is a word that modifies a noun (or pronoun), for example: a *horrible* movie, a *funny* book, or a *delicious* burger. Counting adjectives can determine what type of language is being used, i.e. opinions tend to include more adjectives than facts.

You could later extend this script to count positive adjectives (*great, awesome, happy*, etc.) versus negative adjectives (*boring, lame, sad*, etc.), which could be used to analyze the sentiment of tweets or reviews about a product or movie, for example. This script provides data that can in turn inform decisions related to that product or movie.

Step 3 — Tokenizing Sentences

Create the script and store with .py extension with following code:.

from nltk.corpus import twitter_samples

tweets = twitter_samples.strings('positive_tweets.json')

When we first load our list of tweets, each tweet is represented as one string. Before we can determine which words in our tweets are adjectives or nouns, we first need to tokenize our tweets.

Tokenization is the act of breaking up a sequence of strings into pieces such as words, keywords, phrases, symbols and other elements, which are called *tokens*. Let's create a new variable called tweets_tokens, to which we will assign the tokenized list of tweets:

tweets_tokens = twitter_samples.tokenized('positive_tweets.json')

This new variable, tweets_tokens, is a list where each element in the list is a list of tokens. Now that we have the tokens of each tweet we can tag the tokens with the appropriate POS tags.

Step 4 — Tagging Sentences

In order to access NLTK's POS tagger, we'll need to import it.
from nltk.corpus import twitter_samples
from nltk.tag import pos_tag_sents

tweets = twitter_samples.strings('positive_tweets.json')
tweets_tokens = twitter_samples.tokenized('positive_tweets.json')

Now, we can tag each of our tokens. NLTK allows us to do it all at once using: pos_tag_sents(). We are going to create a new variable tweets_tagged, which we will use to store our tagged lists. This new line can be put directly at the end of our current script:

tweets_tagged = pos_tag_sents(tweets_tokens)

To get an idea of what tagged tokens look like, here is what the first element in our tweets_tagged list looks like:

[(u'#FollowFriday', 'JJ'), (u'@France_Inte', 'NNP'), (u'@PKuchly57', 'NNP'), (u'@Milipol_Paris', 'NNP'), (u'for', 'IN'), (u'being', 'VBG'), (u'top', 'JJ'), (u'engaged', 'VBN'), (u'members', 'NNS'), (u'in', 'IN'), (u'my', 'PRP$'), (u'community', 'NN'), (u'this', 'DT'), (u'week', 'NN'), (u':)', 'NN')]

We can see that our tweet is represented as a list and for each token we have information about its POS tag. Each token/tag pair is saved as a tuple.
In NLTK, the abbreviation for adjective is JJ.
The NLTK tagger marks singular nouns (NN) with different tags than plural nouns (NNS). To simplify, we will only count singular nouns by keeping track of the NN tag.
In the next step we will count how many times JJ and NN appear throughout our corpus.

Step 5 — Counting POS Tags

We will keep track of how many times JJ and NN appear using an accumulator (count) variable, which we will continuously add to every time we find a tag. First let's create our count at the bottom of our script, which we will first set to zero.

```
from nltk.corpus import twitter_samples
from nltk.tag import pos_tag_sents
tweets = twitter_samples.strings('positive_tweets.json')
tweets_tokens = twitter_samples.tokenized('positive_tweets.json')

JJ_count = 0
NN_count = 0
```

After we create the variables, we'll create two for loops. The first loop will iterate through each tweet in the list. The second loop will iterate through each token/tag pair in each tweet. For each pair, we will look up the tag using the appropriate tuple index.

We will then check to see if the tag matches either the string 'JJ' or 'NN' by using conditional statements. If the tag is a match we will add (+= 1) to the appropriate accumulator.

```
from nltk.corpus import twitter_samples
from nltk.tag import pos_tag_sents
tweets = twitter_samples.strings('positive_tweets.json')
tweets_tokens = twitter_samples.tokenized('positive_tweets.json')

JJ_count = 0
NN_count = 0

for tweet in tweets_tagged:
    for pair in tweet:
        tag = pair[1]
        if tag == 'JJ':
            JJ_count += 1
        elif tag == 'NN':
            NN_count += 1
```

After the two loops are complete, we should have the total count for adjectives and nouns in our corpus. To see how many adjectives and nouns our script found, we'll add print statements to the end of the script.

```
print('Total number of adjectives = ', JJ_count)
print('Total number of nouns = ', NN_count)
```

At this point, our program will be able to output the number of adjectives and nouns that were found in the corpus.

Step 6 — Running the NLP Script

Save your abc.py file and run it to see how many adjectives and nouns we find:
python abc.py

Output
Total number of adjectives = 6094
Total number of nouns = 13180

Finished Code

For our finished code, we should add some comments to make it easier for others and our future self to follow. Our script looks like this:

abc.py
```
# Import data and tagger
from nltk.corpus import twitter_samples
from nltk.tag import pos_tag_sents

# Load tokenized tweets
tweets_tokens = twitter_samples.tokenized('positive_tweets.json')

# Tag tagged tweets
tweets_tagged = pos_tag_sents(tweets_tokens)

# Set accumulators
JJ_count = 0
NN_count = 0

# Loop through list of tweets
for tweet in tweets_tagged:
    for pair in tweet:
        tag = pair[1]
        if tag == 'JJ':
            JJ_count += 1
        elif tag == 'NN':
            NN_count += 1

# Print total numbers for each adjectives and nouns
print('Total number of adjectives = ', JJ_count)
print('Total number of nouns = ', NN_count)
```

DATA PRE PROCESSING USING NLTK

Split into Sentences

Some modeling tasks prefer input to be in the form of paragraphs or sentences, such as word2vec. You could first split your text into sentences, split each sentence into words, then save each sentence to file, one per line.
NLTK provides the *sent_tokenize()* function to split text into sentences.

[Python for Data Analysis]   110

The example below loads the "abc.*txt*" file into memory, splits it into sentences, and prints the first sentence.

```
# load data
filename = 'abc.txt'
file = open(filename, 'rt')
text = file.read()
file.close()
# split into sentences
from nltk import sent_tokenize
sentences = sent_tokenize(text)
print(sentences[0])
```

Split into Words

NLTK provides a function called *word_tokenize()* for splitting strings into tokens (nominally words).
It splits tokens based on white space and punctuation. For example, commas and periods are taken as separate tokens. Contractions are split apart (e.g. *"What's"* becomes *"What"* *"'s"*). Quotes are kept, and so on

```
# load data
filename = 'abc.txt'
file = open(filename, 'rt')
text = file.read()
file.close()
# split into words
from nltk.tokenize import word_tokenize
tokens = word_tokenize(text)
print(tokens[:100])
```

Filter Out Punctuation

We can filter out all tokens that we are not interested in, such as all standalone punctuation.
This can be done by iterating over all tokens and only keeping those tokens that are all alphabetic. Python has the function isalpha() that can be used. For example:

```
# load data
filename = 'abc.txt'
file = open(filename, 'rt')
text = file.read()
file.close()
# split into words
from nltk.tokenize import word_tokenize
```

[Python for Data Analysis]   111

```
tokens = word_tokenize(text)
# remove all tokens that are not alphabetic
words = [word for word in tokens if word.isalpha()]
print(words[:100])
```

Filter out Stop Words (and Pipeline)

Stop words are those words that do not contribute to the deeper meaning of the phrase.
They are the most common words such as: *"the"*, *"a"*, and *"is"*.
For some applications like documentation classification, it may make sense to remove stop words.
NLTK provides a list of commonly agreed upon stop words for a variety of languages, such as English. They can be loaded as follows:

```
from nltk.corpus import stopwords
stop_words = stopwords.words('english')
print(stop_words)
```
We can see the complete list as follows as output:
['i', 'me', 'my', 'myself', 'we', 'our', 'ours', 'ourselves', 'you', 'your', 'yours', 'yourself', 'yourselves', 'he', 'him', 'his', 'himself', 'she', 'her', 'hers', 'herself', 'it', 'its', 'itself', 'they', 'them', 'their', 'theirs', 'themselves', 'what', 'which', 'who', 'whom', 'this', 'that', 'these', 'those', 'am', 'is', 'are', 'was', 'were', 'be', 'been', 'being', 'have', 'has', 'had', 'having', 'do', 'does', 'did', 'doing', 'a', 'an', 'the', 'and', 'but', 'if', 'or', 'because', 'as', 'until', 'while', 'of', 'at', 'by', 'for', 'with', 'about', 'against', 'between', 'into', 'through', 'during', 'before', 'after', 'above', 'below', 'to', 'from', 'up', 'down', 'in', 'out', 'on', 'off', 'over', 'under', 'again', 'further', 'then', 'once', 'here', 'there', 'when', 'where', 'why', 'how', 'all', 'any', 'both', 'each', 'few', 'more', 'most', 'other', 'some', 'such', 'no', 'nor', 'not', 'only', 'own', 'same', 'so', 'than', 'too', 'very', 's', 't', 'can', 'will', 'just', 'don', 'should', 'now', 'd', 'll', 'm', 'o', 're', 've', 'y', 'ain', 'aren', 'couldn', 'didn', 'doesn', 'hadn', 'hasn', 'haven', 'isn', 'ma', 'mightn', 'mustn', 'needn', 'shan', 'shouldn', 'wasn', 'weren', 'won', 'wouldn']

Stem Words

Stemming refers to the process of reducing each word to its root or base.
For example *"fishing," "fished," "fisher"* all reduce to the stem *"fish."*
Some applications, like document classification, may benefit from stemming in order to both reduce the vocabulary and to focus on the sense or sentiment of a document rather than deeper meaning.

There are many stemming algorithms, although a popular and long-standing method is the Porter Stemming algorithm. This method is available in NLTK via the PorterStemmer class.

For example:
```
# load data
filename = 'abc.txt'
file = open(filename, 'rt')
text = file.read()
file.close()
# split into words
from nltk.tokenize import word_tokenize
tokens = word_tokenize(text)
# stemming of words
from nltk.stem.porter import PorterStemmer
porter = PorterStemmer()
stemmed = [porter.stem(word) for word in tokens]
print(stemmed[:100])
```

Example of data preparation:-
This example loads the text, Split into tokens, Convert to lowercase, Remove punctuation from each token, Filter out remaining tokens that are not alphabetic and Filter out tokens that are stop words.

```
# load data
filename = 'abc.txt'
file = open(filename, 'rt')
text = file.read()
file.close()
# split into words
from nltk.tokenize import word_tokenize
tokens = word_tokenize(text)
# convert to lower case
tokens = [w.lower() for w in tokens]
# remove punctuation from each word
import string
table = str.maketrans('', '', string.punctuation)
stripped = [w.translate(table) for w in tokens]
# remove remaining tokens that are not alphabetic
words = [word for word in stripped if word.isalpha()]
# filter out stop words
from nltk.corpus import stopwords
stop_words = set(stopwords.words('english'))
```

```
words = [w for w in words if not w in stop_words]
print(words[:100])
```

5.3 Viva Questions

Q1. Compare Java & Python

Criteria	Java	Python
Ease of use	Good	Very Good
Speed of coding	Average	Excellent
Data types	Static typed	Dynamically typed
Data Science & machine learning applications	Average	Very Good

Q2. Name some of the features of Python.

Following are some of the salient features of python –
- It supports functional and structured programming methods as well as OOP.
- It can be used as a scripting language or can be compiled to byte-code for building large applications.
- It provides very high-level dynamic data types and supports dynamic type checking.
- It supports automatic garbage collection.
- It can be easily integrated with C, C++, COM, ActiveX, CORBA, and Java.

Q3. Explain how Python does Compile-time and Run-time code checking?

Python performs some amount of compile-time checking, but most of the checks such as type, name, etc are postponed until code execution. Consequently, if the Python code references a user-defined function that does not exist, the code will compile successfully. In fact, the code will fail with an exception only when the code execution path references the function which does not exists.

Q4. Explain how to overload constructors or methods in Python.

Python's constructor – _init_ () is a first method of a class. Whenever we try to instantiate a object __init__() is automatically invoked by python to initialize members of an object.

Q5. Which statement of Python is used whenever a statement is required syntactically but the program needs no action?

Pass – is no-operation / action statement in Python
If we want to load a module or open a file, and even if the requested module/file does not exist, we want to continue with other tasks. In such a scenario, use try-except block with pass statement in the except block.
Eg:
 try:import mymodulemyfile = open("C:\myfile.csv")except:pass

Q6. Name the File-related modules in Python?

Python provides libraries / modules with functions that enable you to manipulate text files and binary files on file system. Using them you can create files, update their contents, copy, and delete files. The libraries are : os, os.path, and shutil. Here, os and os.path – modules include functions for accessing the file system

Q7. Explain the shortest way to open a text file and display its contents.?
The shortest way to open a text file is by using "with" command as follows:
with open("file-name", "r") as fp:
fileData = fp.read()
#to print the contents of the file print(fileData)

Q8. When does a dictionary is used instead of a list?

Dictionaries – are best suited when the data is labelled, i.e., the data is a record with field names.
lists – are better option to store collections of un-labelled items say all the files and sub directories in a folder.Generally Search operation on dictionary object is faster than searching a list object.

Q9. How many kinds of sequences are supported by Python? What are they?

Python supports 7 sequence types. They are str, list, tuple, unicode, bytearray, xrange, and buffer. where xrange is deprecated in python 3.5.X.

Q10. How do you perform pattern matching in Python? Explain

Regular Expressions/REs/ regexes enable us to specify expressions that can match specific "parts" of a given string. For instance, we can define a regular expression to match a single character or a digit, a telephone number, or an email address, etc.

Q11. Name few Python modules for Statistical, Numerical and scientific computations ?

numPy – this module provides an array/matrix type, and it is useful for doing computations on arrays. scipy – this module provides methods for doing numeric integrals, solving differential equations, etc pylab – is a module for generating and saving plots
matplotlib – used for managing data and generating plots.

Q12. Is Python object oriented? what is object oriented programming?
Yes. Python is Object Oriented Programming language. OOP is the programming paradigm based on classes and instances of those classes called objects. The features of OOP are:
Encapsulation, Data Abstraction, Inheritance, Polymorphism.

Q13. How instance variables are different from class variables?

Instance variables: are the variables in an object that have values that are local to that object. Two objects of the same class maintain distinct values for their variables. These variables are accessed with "object-name.instancevariable-name".
class variables: these are the variables of class. All the objects of the same class will share value of "Class variables. They are accessed with their class name alone as "class- name.classvariable-name". If you change the value of a class variable in one object, its new value is visible among all other objects of the same class. In the Java world, a variable that is declared as static is a class variable.

Q14. Explain different ways to trigger / raise exceptions in your python script ?

The following are the two possible ways by which you can trigger an exception in your Python script. They are:
raise — it is used to manually raise an exception general-form:
raise exception-name ("message to be conveyed")
Eg: >>> voting_age = 15
>>> if voting_age < 18: raise ValueError("voting age should be atleast 18 and above") output: ValueError: voting age should be atleast 18 and above 2. assert statement assert statements are used to tell your program to test that condition attached to assert keyword, and trigger an exception whenever the condition becomes false. Eg: >>> a = -10
>>> assert a > 0 #to raise an exception whenever a is a negative number output: AssertionError
Another way of raising and exception can be done by making a programming mistake, but that's not

usually a good way of triggering an exception.

Q15. Does Python supports interfaces like in Java? Discuss.

Python does not provide interfaces like in Java. Abstract Base Class (ABC) and its feature are provided by the Python's "abc" module. Abstract Base Class is a mechanism for specifying what methods must be implemented by its implementation subclasses. The use of ABC'c provides a sort of "understanding" about methods and their expected behaviour. This module was made available from Python 2.7 version onwards.

Q16. Differentiate between .py and .pyc files?

Both .py and .pyc files holds the byte code. ".pyc" is a compiled version of Python file. This file is automatically generated by Python to improve performance. The .pyc file is having byte code which is platform independent and can be executed on any operating system that supports .pyc format.

Q17. Name few Python Web Frameworks for developing web applications?

There are various web frameworks provided by Python. They are
web2py – it is the simplest of all the web frameworks used for developing web applications.
cherryPy – it is a Python-based Object oriented Web framework.
Flask – it is a Python-based micro-framework for designing and developing web applications.

Q18. How will you remove an object from a list?
list.remove(obj) – Removes object obj from list.

Q19. What is the output of L[1:] if L = [1,2,3]?
2, 3, Slicing fetches sections.

Q20. What is the difference between del() and remove() methods of list?

To remove a list element, you can use either the del statement if you know exactly which element(s) you are deleting or the remove() method if you do not know.

Q21. What is the output of print tuple + tinytuple if tuple = ('abcd', 786 , 2.23, 'john', 70.2) and tinytuple = (123, 'john')?

[Python for Data Analysis]   117

It will print concatenated tuples. Output would be ('abcd', 786, 2.23, 'john', 70.200000000000003, 123, 'john').

Q22. What is the difference between tuples and lists in Python?

The main differences between lists and tuples are – Lists are enclosed in brackets ([ ]) and their elements and size can be changed, while tuples are enclosed in parentheses (( )) and cannot be updated. Tuples can be thought of as read-only lists.

Q23. Is python a case sensitive language?
Yes! Python is a case sensitive programming language.

References:

http://www.i-programmer.info/programming/python/
https://docs.scipy.org/doc/numpy-dev/user/quickstart.html
http://www.numpy.org/
http://matplotlib.org/users/pyplot_tutorial.html
http://pandas.pydata.org/pandas-docs/stable/visualization.html
http://www.afterhoursprogramming.com/tutorial/Python/Reading-Files/
https://www.analyticsvidhya.com/blog/2016/06/quick-guide-build-recommendation-engine-python/
https://t.co/Ke67eousns
http://www.geeksforgeeks.org/twitter-sentiment-analysis-using-python/

Printed in Great Britain
by Amazon